HBR'S 10 MUST READS

W0010200

On
**Nonprofits
and the
Social Sectors**

HBR's 10 Must Reads series is the definitive collection of ideas and best practices for aspiring and experienced leaders alike. These books offer essential reading selected from the pages of *Harvard Business Review* on topics critical to the success of every manager.

Titles include:

HBR's 10 Must Reads 2015
HBR's 10 Must Reads 2016
HBR's 10 Must Reads 2017
HBR's 10 Must Reads 2018
HBR's 10 Must Reads 2019
HBR's 10 Must Reads 2020
HBR's 10 Must Reads for CEOs
HBR's 10 Must Reads for New Managers
HBR's 10 Must Reads on AI, Analytics, and the New Machine Age
HBR's 10 Must Reads on Business Model Innovation
HBR's 10 Must Reads on Change Management
HBR's 10 Must Reads on Collaboration
HBR's 10 Must Reads on Communication
HBR's 10 Must Reads on Diversity
HBR's 10 Must Reads on Emotional Intelligence
HBR's 10 Must Reads on Entrepreneurship and Startups
HBR's 10 Must Reads on Innovation
HBR's 10 Must Reads on Leadership
HBR's 10 Must Reads on Leadership for Healthcare
HBR's 10 Must Reads on Leadership Lessons from Sports
HBR's 10 Must Reads on Making Smart Decisions
HBR's 10 Must Reads on Managing Across Cultures
HBR's 10 Must Reads on Managing People
HBR's 10 Must Reads on Managing Yourself
HBR's 10 Must Reads on Mental Toughness
HBR's 10 Must Reads on Negotiation
HBR's 10 Must Reads on Nonprofits and the Social Sectors
HBR's 10 Must Reads on Reinventing HR

On
Nonprofits
and the
Social Sectors

HARVARD BUSINESS REVIEW PRESS
Boston, Massachusetts

Library of Congress Cataloging-in-Publication Data

Title: HBR's 10 must reads on nonprofits and the social sectors.
Other titles: HBR's ten must reads on nonprofits and the social sectors | Harvard Business Review's 10 must reads on nonprofits and social sectors | Nonprofits and the social sectors | HBR's 10 must reads (Series)
Description: Boston, Massachusetts : Harvard Business Review Press, [2019] | Series: HBR's 10 must reads
Identifiers: LCCN 2018052901 | ISBN 9781633696907 (pbk.)
Subjects: LCSH: Nonprofit organizations—Management. | Humanitarianism. | Leadership.
Classification: LCC HD62.6 .H425 2019 | DDC 658/.048—dc23 LC record available at https://lccn.loc.gov/2018052901

ISBN: 9781633696907
eISBN: 9781633696914

Contents

**HBR'S
10
MUST
READS**

On
Nonprofits
and the
Social Sectors

Lofty Missions, Down-to-Earth Plans

by V. Kasturi Rangan

MOST OF THE NONPROFITS OPERATING today make program decisions based on a mission rather than on a strategy. In fact, many nonprofits don't have a strategy at all. They rally under the banner of a particular cause, be it "Fight homelessness" or "End hunger." And then, since that cause is so worthwhile, nonprofits support any program that's related to it—even if only tangentially. While it's hard to fault people for trying to improve the state of the world, this approach is misguided. Acting without a clear long-term strategy can stretch an agency's core capabilities and push it in unintended directions.

Consider, for example, the work of SOS Kinderdorf, headquartered in Innsbruck, Austria. Founded in 1949 by Hermann Gmeiner to "provide orphaned, abandoned, and destitute children with a new and permanent home, and lay a sound foundation for a useful and productive life," SOS Kinderdorf currently operates more than 425 children's villages in 131 countries, mostly in Africa, Asia, and Latin America.

Gmeiner envisioned a children's village that would be more personal than a traditional orphanage. At the outset, each village

1

consisted of a cluster of ten to 15 homes, and each home housed six to eight children, selected by age to approximate sibling patterns. Every family was cared for by a "mother"—a carefully selected single woman who received training in home economics, cooking, family health, and education.

Before long, this straightforward program became more complex. Kinderdorf's managers realized that the children needed more than a secure and loving home: They needed education and vocational training. But in most countries where Kinderdorf operated, decent schools were unavailable or inaccessible. So the organization decided to open kindergartens in its villages. Then it started K-12 schools and vocational training centers. Because quality K-12 schools would not be viable without the scale to accommodate a couple of hundred children across the various grade levels, Kinderdorf opened them to children from neighboring communities, some of whom paid tuition. Along with the revenue this decision generated, it allowed the Kinderdorf children to become integrated with the larger community. When Kinderdorf added medical centers to its villages, they, too, were made available to neighboring communities. By 2000, nearly 40% of Kinderdorf's annual budget was spent on schools, medical centers, and other such services, and only 60% on the core services concerned with food, housing, and clothing.

In one way, it made perfect sense for Kinderdorf's trustees and senior managers to broaden the nonprofit's range of activities. The children in their care wouldn't be able to lead productive lives without an education, vocational training, health care, career placement, and even (in some countries) arranged marriages, when they reached adulthood.

When taken to its logical conclusion, though, this kind of expansion could have continued until the organization became too stretched to be effective in addressing the core dimensions of its broad mission. For instance, what was to keep Kinderdorf from providing housing for women and children displaced by natural calamities or civil war? That's exactly how country managers in India interpreted the mission in 1996, when they chose to participate in

Idea in Brief

Most nonprofits make program decisions based on a mission rather than a strategy. They rally under the banner of a particular cause, be it "fight homelessness" or "end hunger." And since their causes are so worthwhile, they support any programs that are related—even tangentially—to their core missions.

It's hard to fault people for trying to improve the state of the world, but that approach to making decisions is misguided. Acting without a clear long-term strategy can stretch an agency's core capabilities and push it in unintended directions.

The fundamental problem is that many nonprofits don't have a strategy; instead, they have a mission and a portfolio of programs. But they hardly make deliberate decisions about which programs to run, which to drop, and which to turn down for funding. What most nonprofits call "strategy" is really just an intensive exercise in resource allocation and program management.

This article outlines for nonprofits a four-step process for developing strategy. The first step is to create a broad, inspiring mission statement. The second step is to translate that core mission into a smaller, quantifiable operational mission. For instance, an agency whose core mission is to fight homelessness must decide if its focus is rural or urban and if it should concentrate on low-income housing loans or on establishing more shelters. The third step is to create a strategy platform; that is, the nonprofit decides how it will achieve its operational mission. Decisions about funding and about client, program, and organizational development are all made here. Once that platform is established, the nonprofit is ready to move to step four—making reasoned, strategic decisions about which programs to run and how to run them.

The agency that follows these steps will improve its focus and its effectiveness at fulfilling its mission.

disaster relief after an earthquake razed the town of Latur. But the dimensions of service creation and delivery are entirely different in the stable environment of a children's village from what they are when looking after families displaced by calamities—even though both involve taking care of orphaned children. Or what's to prevent Kinderdorf from caring for children orphaned by AIDS? Nothing. In fact, that is its mission, but should it be drawn into the care of families struck by AIDS in order to ensure a psychologically smooth transition for the children when their parents ultimately succumb to the disease?

Expanding into emergency relief or AIDS rehabilitation is perfectly consistent with the organization's mission. But even a superb organization like Kinderdorf probably can't function effectively in such a broad range of health, education, and community services. Like all nonprofits, it must decide how much of a stretch is necessary—even visionary—and how much is a drift and a drain.

Mission Stick Versus Market Pull

Nonprofits have strong reasons to stay loyal to their missions. After all, the mission is what inspires founders to create the organization, and it draws board members, staff, donors, and volunteers to become involved. What's more, the founders often deliberately ensure that their original vision is embraced by the next generation of leaders. At Kinderdorf, for example, Gmeiner groomed Helmut Kutin as his successor. Kutin had come to one of the villages as an orphan at 12 and had grown up to become a very successful travel industry executive. Kutin in turn chose as secretary general Richard Pichler, a computer science professional who had come to the village at nine. Kutin and Pichler, both products of the system, reflected its core values and culture; they didn't know otherwise. This also holds true of key leaders, board members, and volunteers at other nonprofits. With such similar self-perpetuating representations of an organization's culture at different levels, the core mission becomes cemented into the consciousness of the entire organization. But sometimes that "mission stickiness" is detrimental. Nonprofits risk becoming rigid and falling behind the changing times.

Founded in 1916, Planned Parenthood Federation of America is the world's oldest voluntary reproductive health care organization. It champions individuals' fundamental rights to manage their fertility, regardless of income level, marital status, age, national origin, or residence. By the early 1990s, Planned Parenthood had a network of more than 100 affiliates, and revenues exceeding $400 million. Then suddenly its market environment shifted: Managed care broke the virtual monopoly of indemnity plans in the health insurance industry, and because these managed-care plans covered a broader range of reproductive services, Planned Parenthood's earned revenue declined. At the same time, many uninsured patients, who could not afford to pay, had no choice but to rely on Planned Parenthood for reproductive health services.

In 1993, Planned Parenthood commissioned a task force to consider its response to the decrease in paying customers and increase in nonpaying ones. The task force proposed a bold step forward into general women-centered health care from its narrow focus on reproductive health, and it also proposed consolidation moves to garner a better position in the new managed-care market.

Within four months' time, however, Planned Parenthood affiliates rolled back the task force's two key recommendations—the expanded approach to women's health care and recommendations to consolidate smaller affiliates. These actions were seen as diluting the organization's mission of supporting and protecting abortion rights and of providing an environment that allowed all—but especially indigent—women to seek such services. The change program, many thought, was too responsive to the shifting commercial winds of Planned Parenthood's environment. For good or for bad, mission stickiness won out.

Yet even as nonprofits are stuck to their mission, they are also pulled by market forces. The need to attract new donors often compels nonprofits to take on programs that don't fit their existing capabilities and expertise well. Consider New York–based STRIVE (Support and Training Result In Valuable Employees), for instance. It distinguished itself in the early 1990s with impressive and measurable results in the relatively narrow niche of soft-skills job training (such as interviewing abilities) and in the placement of a highly self-selective group of acutely disadvantaged inner-city residents in entry-level employment. The agency's success attracted private

5

funding for core programs and operations, and its reputation for delivering results helped attract a large Ford Foundation short-term grant. This grant was tied to a program that provided hard-skills training (such as computer literacy) to place clients in career-path positions. And while it was arguably consistent with STRIVE's mission of helping unemployed inner-city residents gain self-sufficiency through work, almost overnight the grant significantly broadened the organization's focus, accounting for one-third of the budget and personnel. Naturally, some of these extensions proved very challenging.

Small, cash-strapped nonprofits often find that the most accessible funding is restricted to specific initiatives, programs, and contracts. They accept them because they nominally fall within the organization's broad mission statement, but they are much better aligned with the donor's strategy than with the nonprofit's. Because the funds barely cover the direct costs of the additional activity, much less the indirect costs, the nonprofit reenters the funding market again and again, each time as a bigger, less focused, and more cash-starved entity.

Large nonprofits aren't immune to market pull, either. In fact, it is precisely because agencies such as Kinderdorf, the United Way, and the American Red Cross are so successful that they shoulder more demands from their donors and trustees to take on programs that address the core mission—in however roundabout a manner.

The combination of stickiness to the mission and stretchiness to market demands can undermine a nonprofit's effectiveness. The stretchiness keeps it very busy on a day-today basis; it's constantly executing programs and working to raise funds. But in a strategic sense, the organization moves very slowly because the stickiness holds it in place. Before it can move forward, it must unstick the inertia at its center and then creep forward one step at a time, carrying with it all its baggage.

As a consequence of this stick-and-stretch syndrome, nonprofits often develop anaerobic life styles. At one extreme is the bloated bureaucracy: It may have some hardworking parts, but as a whole, it's slow moving and survives because of mission legitimacy, not mission performance. At the other is the ever-busy nonprofit characterized by action paralysis. The organization is so busy executing the day-to-day stuff, raising money, implementing programs, and so on, that it never steps back to consider the full implications of its actions.

A Four-Step Strategy Process

The fundamental problem is that these agencies don't have a strategy. They have a mission, and they have a portfolio of programs, but they have hardly made any deliberate decisions regarding which programs to run and which to drop or turn down. What most nonprofits consider strategy is really just intensive resource allocation and program management activity.

Nonprofits don't have the discipline of the bottom line and of performance-obsessed capital markets, so they can go for years without having to make strategic choices. Moreover, because neither the nonprofits nor their funding sources are especially skilled at measuring results, it's easy for them to fall into a vicious cycle of ineffectiveness that can take years to become apparent. Only a grave crisis, a visionary leader, or an outsider (such as a board member) would be able to highlight the need for strategic deliberation and redirection.

Without such a spur, large nonprofits and foundations rely on policy guidelines that determine the appropriate proposals or programs to support. These rules and principles provide a rationale for how and why the programs fit the organizations' broad mission. But that is not strategy. Strategy is about future action, not historical justification. Small nonprofits, for their part, do not have the luxury of choice. They must instead go where the money is, as long as it is broadly consistent with the mission. Both large and small nonprofits are overly busy emphasizing mission fit and program delivery.

Think of strategy formulation as a stairway linking the organization's core mission to its programs and activities.[1] (See the exhibit "The strategy stairway.") To create a strategy that is both effective and measurable, nonprofits first need to translate their core mission into a narrower, quantifiable operational mission. Next, the nonprofit needs to convert the operational mission into a strategy platform. Only then can it make reasoned and strategic decisions about which programs to run and how to run them.

Step 1: The mission statement

This statement tends to be broad and far-reaching and usually identifies the customer need the organization attempts to serve, such as hunger, homelessness, or unemployment. The purpose of the mission statement is to inspire. Its credibility lies in the significance and scope of the problem it has identified. A powerful and compelling long-term goal will draw the attention of funders, workers, and volunteers. Habitat for Humanity International's goal is "to eliminate poverty housing and homelessness from the face of the earth [and] put the subject of inadequate housing in the hearts and minds of people." The mission tells you the nature of the problem, but it doesn't identify how Habitat will address that need or how much of it will be served by the organization.

Over the years, the core mission does not change much. That's because the fundamental problem that a nonprofit addresses rarely disappears entirely, although it may decrease in size and scope. (Sometimes, however, when the problem is well under control, a nonprofit may declare victory—as in 1958 when the March of Dimes changed its mission to fighting birth defects after the Salk vaccine eradicated polio.)

Step 2: The operational mission

This step brings the lofty, inspirational mission into the realm of quantitative goals. While the big mission should be broad enough to guide action through periods of organizational and environmental change, the operational mission must be narrow enough to allow the organization to trace its impact. The organization's work should always be measurable, even if it must use proxies to do so. Habitat for Humanity, for example, tracks not only the number of homes it has built, but in some areas it also estimates the extent of poverty housing yet to be eliminated.

The operational mission answers the following provocative questions: What are you going to do about this problem? What is your unique role? Will you fight homelessness by, for instance, building homes, reforming public housing, or boosting no-interest housing loans for the poor? Will you address rural or urban

The strategy stairway

Too many nonprofits rely on their core mission to guide their program delivery decisions. They miss two critical intermediate steps: formulating an operational mission and devising a strategy platform. Without those steps, nonprofits easily fall prey to the stick-and-stretch syndrome.

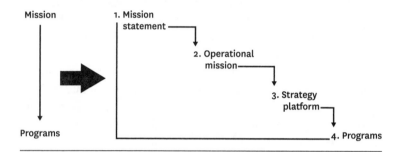

homelessness or both? The best answers specify the form of engagement through which the organization will have the most impact in the foreseeable future, given its expected resources and capabilities.

While the big mission is usually sacrosanct, the operational mission should reflect environmental changes that might either constrain or provide new opportunities for accomplishing the overarching mission. In other words, the operational mission should change as the organization learns more about the environment and its mission performance.

The Nature Conservancy, for instance, changed its strategic direction when it realized that buying up land to protect rare species wasn't doing enough to fulfill its big mission of preserving plants and special habitats. The Nature Conservancy began its work by purchasing or managing large tracts of land that it could protect. At one point, it was protecting more than 10 million acres. Its revenues by the late 1990s were about $575 million, and it was growing at 18% annually. The former CEO, the late John Sawhill, described the issue this way: "From an institutional perspective,

9

the traditional measures of bucks and acres seemed to tell a story of uninterrupted success. But in the backs of our minds there lurked a nagging question. How good are bucks and acres in terms of assessing concrete, measurable progress toward our mission of conserving biodiversity?"

The Nature Conservancy recognized that it couldn't operate successfully if it ignored the communities and businesses surrounding its land. For instance, the bog turtle population of Schenob Brook Preserve in Sheffield, Massachusetts, was declining several years after the Nature Conservancy acquired the property because activities outside the area affected the water the turtles depended on. According to Sawhill, "It became clear that we needed to influence land use in larger areas . . . to ensure that the economic and recreational activities going on outside the preserves don't undermine the balance of life inside them."

So while the organization remained true to its core mission, it revised its operational implementation: "The mission of The Nature Conservancy is to preserve plants, animals and natural communities that represent the diversity of life on Earth by protecting the lands and waters they need to survive." This directional adjustment spurred the Nature Conservancy to devise ways to collaborate with communities, governments, and businesses rather than simply trying to own all the land all the time. Obviously, with such a change in approach, the measures changed as well.

Step 3: The strategy platform
This delineates how the operational mission will be achieved, including which programs to run and how to run them. The strategy platform consists of four important components: client and market development, program and service development and delivery, funder and donor development, and organization development and governance. (See the exhibit "Blueprint of a strategy platform.") Each one should directly relate to the operating mission and should dovetail with the other components. Most important, every program should correspond to its appropriate strategy platform component.

Blueprint of a strategy platform

A nonprofit's strategy platform outlines how the organization will fulfill its operational mission—in terms of funding, organization, client, and program development. Once the platform is in place, the nonprofit will be able to make reasoned, strategic decisions about which programs to run and how to run them.

A prime example of a well-conceived strategy platform is that of Aravind Eye Hospital in India. The hospital, founded by Dr. Venkataswamy in 1976, began with just 20 beds and today has more than 2,500 in a four-hospital network. Its core mission is to provide quality eye-care services to all those who need them without regard to their ability to pay. Its operating mission revolves around cataract surgery, since cataracts cause roughly 75% of the 30 million cases of blindness in India. It has developed a unique, self-sustaining strategy platform that allowed it in 2002 to screen nearly 800,000 patients free of charge (and another 600,000 for a fee). The hospital has also provided free surgical care to 150,000 patients (and another 50,000 for a fee) and still has made a $3 million contribution to its bottom line. It hasn't been this successful by luck or happenstance. The four areas of Aravind's strategy platform work together like a well-oiled machine.

Client and market development. Instead of waiting for those in need to come to its door, Aravind holds eye camps in rural areas to find patients. Medical teams work closely with community leaders and service groups to set up camps that screen hundreds of people in a single day. Free screening camps are held every day, and while Aravind provides the staff and the medical equipment, community partners like the Lions Club, charitable organizations, or local philanthropists organize and publicize the camp and provide food and busing for those selected for surgery.

Program and service development and delivery. Aravind's process of readying the patient for surgery, performing the surgery, and getting the patient through recovery is all configured like a modern assembly line. So while the average ophthalmologist in India performs about 200 cataract surgeries a year, an Aravind doctor performs about 1,500—an efficiency multiple of 7.5. To keep the cost of surgery low, the hospital initially offered its free-care patients intracapsular surgery, which was performed without an operating microscope. These patients didn't receive a $30 intraocular lens, which cost too much for the hospital to absorb. But Aravind's mission was to provide the highest quality care to poor patients, so in 1992, it decided to produce intraocular lenses in its own facility, Auro-Lab. It cut the cost of each lens to just $7, so by 2002, all patients were able to receive it.

Generally speaking, a nonprofit developing a model for program delivery should ask such questions as the following: What are the distinctive aspects of the service delivery model? What are the leverage points? Is there a more effective or efficient way to deliver the programs? What resources, capabilities, and systems are needed?

Funder and donor development. Paying patients make up approximately 40% of the total pool. The paying segment is crucial to Aravind's strategy for two reasons: These patients pay market prices for their eye care because Aravind is the quality leader in its field, and the income generated subsidizes the organization's core mission. Second, paying clients set high demands on quality care, and those standards are used as a benchmark for nonpaying clients as well. Because the paying patients are so central to its funding model, Aravind does give them some special services—hot meals, beds (as opposed to floor mats) in air-conditioned areas, and private bathrooms—but it delivers equal-quality surgery to both client segments.

Because Aravind's paying clients subsidize the nonpaying clients, it avoids some of the critical problems other nonprofits face on this front. Many donors will want to attach strings to their contributions—influencing the nature of the program or starting an entirely new initiative. Before a nonprofit alters its program portfolio, it must evaluate the repercussions such a move would have on the operational mission. If an initiative lies outside the scope of the operational mission, the organization must resist the temptation to cater to donors' wishes.

It may surprise many nonprofits, but donors are frequently quite open to guidance on how to further the cause they feel so passionately about. Even so, it can involve much persuasion and discussion, and unfortunately, too many nonprofits insulate their development arm from their service delivery arm.

Organizational development and governance. Aravind translates its strategy into every organizational system, norm, and value. To reinforce the ideal of quality without prejudice, for instance, doctors rotate between the free and the paying hospitals, and the quality control procedures are identical at both. Moreover, every doctor does outreach work at the eye camps. In addition, all doctors are encouraged to undertake research, and several of them have been sent to the United States and Europe for further training. Each of these HR policies cultivates the pursuit of high-quality care.

Aravind's strategy platform is so successful because each component directly addresses the organization's operational mission. The long hours of work, the intensive outreach, and the adherence to the highest standards of quality are not just good things to do; they are core elements of Aravind's strategy, and each component dovetails with the others.

Consider, for example, how the funding and marketing models work together. Without the earned-income pool of paying patients, market feedback would be muted. If that occurred, the discipline needed to maintain high-quality standards would diminish, and so would the treatment of poor patients. Partly to address the market needs of this funding segment, Aravind offers a comprehensive variety of noncataract specialty clinics. Retinal detachment corrections, vitreous surgery, laser procedures, and other services make up roughly 20% of Aravind's total surgeries. (In other words, the program and service delivery model allows Aravind to maintain its funding model.) Even more important, Aravind's doctors are challenged to master new skills for these other disciplines, which help them remain committed to Aravind (reinforcing the organizational model). Without such intangible benefits, doctors would be apt to give up their work at Aravind and join private clinics for more substantial salaries. Employee churn would affect morale and quality standards and lead to the collapse of this carefully constructed strategy.

Step 4: The choice of programs

Once an organization has the platform for supporting the various strategy components in a coherent way, the day-to-day tasks of choosing which programs to fund and which to cut are much better guided. When a new program appears on the organization's radar, the first question to ask is, How does the program contribute to the appropriate strategy component—funding development, for instance, or operational development?

Say, for example, a foundation approaches the Nature Conservancy to develop a proposal for an advocacy program that focuses on global environmental preservation. The Nature Conservancy has to evaluate whether the program will enhance its operational mission and whether the program is consistent with its strategy goals. In fact, it is not—the Nature Conservancy is a preservation agency, not an advocacy organization, so taking on the program would stretch the nonprofit in a counterproductive direction. Of course, the advocacy activities of institutions like the World Wildlife Fund directly improve the Nature Conservancy's ability to perform its operating mission, but that's why that program is best left to such a collaborator.

It is, of course, possible to make a transition from one operating mission to another. Population Services International (PSI), for example, was originally focused on family planning in developing countries and by 1990 it was one of the leading agencies—in about a dozen countries—of "contraceptive social marketing."

The instruments used to effect a voluntary change in behavior were the classic marketing methods of communication, information, persuasion, and distribution. But during the mid-1990s, the agency's growth in contraceptive social marketing was threatened by a decline in U.S. Agency for International Development funds for family planning. At the same time, HIV/AIDS prevention became an important issue, and many agencies, new and old, staked claims for the available funds. In addition to laying the groundwork for its entry into HIV/AIDS social marketing, PSI decided to expand into a variety of other preventive public health programs. These programs included developing insecticide-treated nets for malaria prevention, iodized products that prevent deformities and IQ loss, water purification products, and prenatal multivitamins.

This entire range of products and services was a perfect fit for PSI's very capable marketing and distribution arm. The transformation of its operational mission increased its revenue base from $3 million in 1987 to about $100 million in 2000. It has enabled a diversification of funding resources, and even though PSI still addresses the core mission of third-world family health, its operating strategy is much broader than family planning. It is now in the business of family health in developing countries.

Putting It All Together

It is important to remember that the stairway is a framework for strategy formulation, not a methodology. For instance, nonprofits still finding their feet in terms of resources will rely on the fourth step—choosing the programs—to drive their day-to-day operations. Nothing is wrong with that, but once a nonprofit matures, the board and management team members must meet to assess the organization's capabilities based on its execution record. Once the nonprofits know what they're good at, they should carve out a tentative operational mission and strategy platform. In other words, the sequence might work as Step 1, 4, 2, then 3. As soon as all the steps have been established, however, it makes sense to follow the sequential cycle that has been laid out here. If an organization hasn't been able to come up with an operating mission and strategy platform within three to five years of its inception, it should probably shut down.

The operating mission should be the anchor of any long-range strategic plan, and the strategy platform should anchor the annual plan—although no step should be considered in isolation. Therefore, long-range discussions would involve Steps 1, 2, and 3 and should be undertaken every three to five years. Senior managers, the board of directors, and key funders all play important roles in this process. But the board owns responsibility for it. The key questions to ask are as follows:

- Is the core mission a statement of an important problem in society (and therefore an opportunity to improve its state of well-being)?

- Does our operational mission contribute to the core mission in a significant way?

- Does our strategy platform contribute to our mission impact? How do we know?

Too often, nonprofit boards punt their responsibility for this crucial process. What passes for a long-range planning exercise is simply the annual event staged on a grander scale. Not only that, but the senior executives who pull the event together often have a vested interest in prolonging the status quo, and the "discussions" turn into much celebration and rationalization—and little reflection and correction.

At its annual planning and review meetings, by contrast, the organization should focus on Steps 2, 3, and 4. Here management and staff play a larger role than board members. After all, many of the questions regarding fit, efficiency, and integration are best addressed by the people on the front lines of day-to-day implementation.

Even so, the board should ask the following questions at these meetings:

- What is the strategy platform?

- Does the organization have a coherent model to execute the strategy?

Unfortunately, nonprofit boards are not very adept at tackling these two important questions. Some board members, who are also the key sources of funds, skip these strategic questions to dive directly into programming details.

Frequently, their funding clout allows them to influence program choices. Board members who don't bring in the money are often viewed as not holding up their end of the bargain, and, add to that, their input isn't taken as seriously. However, because these members have not invested their own resources in the programs, they may actually, in fact, be more objective in assessing a program's fit.

Programs are the critical units around which the organization carries out its work. If a nonprofit doesn't develop the operating mission and the strategy platform in a disciplined way, its management tends to think every program is important. After all, each addresses the core mission in some fashion, so each is justified. But that kind of thinking causes a nonprofit to drift from its original goals. It also contributes to the burnout of executives and staff, who feel as though they are working as hard as they can but see few results for their efforts. They may resist asking the following questions, but it's crucial that they do:

- How effective are our programs?
- How efficiently are they executed?
- Which programs should we drop?
- Which should we seek to add?

If it doesn't ask these tough questions, a nonprofit risks spreading itself too thin. While all programs may address the core mission in some way, their collective impact is severely diluted by a lack of coherence and consistency.

Instead of trying to be all things to all people, nonprofits should pick a niche, craft an operational mission and, flowing from it, formulate a coherent strategy platform. Then it should vigorously pursue those programs that support the logic of the entire strategy. That approach improves nonprofits' chances for changing the world. Unfortunately, too few nonprofits conduct such strategic assessments of their work. There are approximately 1 million nonprofits operating in the United States, and about 5 million nonprofits operating worldwide. A recent estimate put the combined annual 2000 budget of U.S. nonprofits at $600 billion. The framework offered here will help those dollars be spent more effectively.

Originally published in March 2004. Reprint R0403J

Note

1. The phrase "strategy as a stairway" was coined by Robert Burakoff, an independent nonprofit strategy consultant.

What Business Can Learn from Nonprofits

by Peter F. Drucker

Editor's Note: *Peter F. Drucker is widely viewed as the father of modern management thinking. Over a career that spanned eight decades, he was a tireless teacher, consultant, and writer, omnivorous in his attention to both nonprofit and for-profit organizations. Drucker's ideas remain startlingly relevant today. In writing so cogently about the burgeoning phenomenon of the "knowledge worker," he was able to imagine with great accuracy how the balance of power would shift in organizations in the late 20th and early 21st centuries and how organizational structure, focus, and purpose would also change.*

Nonprofit management is not often held up as an exemplar for corporate leaders. Yet in this classic 1989 article, which has already inspired a generation of nonprofit leaders, Drucker argues that nonprofits are true pioneers, leading the way in the motivation and productivity of knowledge workers. And in the areas of strategy and board effectiveness, nonprofits are stronger than most for-profit organizations.

THE GIRL SCOUTS, THE RED CROSS, THE PASTORAL CHURCHES—our nonprofit organizations—are becoming America's management leaders. In two areas, strategy and the effectiveness of the board, they are practicing what most American businesses only preach. And in the most crucial area—the motivation and productivity of knowledge workers—they are truly pioneers, working out the policies and practices that business will have to learn tomorrow.

Few people are aware that the nonprofit sector is by far America's largest employer. Every other adult—a total of 80 million plus people—works as a volunteer, giving on average nearly five hours each week to one or several nonprofit organizations. This is equal to 10 million full-time jobs. Were volunteers paid, their wages, even at minimum rate, would amount to some $150 billion, or 5% of GNP. And volunteer work is changing fast. To be sure, what many do requires little skill or judgment: collecting in the neighborhood for the Community Chest one Saturday afternoon a year, chaperoning youngsters selling Girl Scout cookies door to door, driving old people to the doctor. But more and more volunteers are becoming "unpaid staff," taking over the professional and managerial tasks in their organizations.

Not all nonprofits have been doing well, of course. A good many community hospitals are in dire straits. Traditional churches and synagogues of all persuasions—liberal, conservative, evangelical, fundamentalist—are still steadily losing members. Indeed, the sector overall has not expanded in the last 10 or 15 years, either in terms of the money it raises (when adjusted for inflation) or in the number of volunteers. Yet in its productivity, in the scope of its work and in its contribution to American society, the nonprofit sector has grown tremendously in the last two decades.

The Salvation Army is an example. People convicted to their first prison term in Florida, mostly very poor black or Hispanic youths, are now paroled into the Salvation Army's custody—about 25,000 each year. Statistics show that if these young men and women go to jail the majority will become habitual criminals. But the Salvation Army has been able to rehabilitate 80% of them through a strict work program run largely by volunteers. And the program costs a fraction of what it would to keep the offenders behind bars.

Underlying this program and many other effective nonprofit endeavors is a commitment to management. Twenty years ago, management was a dirty word for those involved in nonprofit organizations. It meant business, and nonprofits prided themselves on being free of the taint of commercialism and above such sordid considerations as the bottom line. Now most of them have learned that nonprofits need management even more than business does, precisely

Idea in Brief

Every year in Florida, some 25,000 young people who have been convicted to their first term in prison enter the Salvation Army's parole program. Statistics show that if these men and women go to jail, the majority will become habitual criminals. The Salvation Army has been able to rehabilitate 80% of them through a strict work program run largely by volunteers. The program costs a fraction of what it would to keep offenders behind bars.

This kind of effectiveness is characteristic of the best nonprofit organizations. Twenty years ago, management was a dirty word in nonprofits. Today they offer best practice in two areas, strategy and effective use of the board. And in the area that presents the biggest challenge

for every enterprise—motivating knowledge workers and raising their productivity—they are truly pioneers.

In successful nonprofit enterprises, well-meaning amateurs are giving way to unpaid staff members, many of whom work as managers and professionals in their for-pay jobs. These people volunteer because they believe in the organization's mission. They stay because the organization knows how to put their competence and knowledge to work. The formula is the same, whether the employer is a church, the Girl Scouts, or a business: give people responsibility for meaningful tasks, hold them accountable for their performance, reward them with training and the chance to take on more demanding assignments.

because they lack the discipline of the bottom line. The nonprofits are, of course, still dedicated to "doing good." But they also realize that good intentions are no substitute for organization and leadership, for accountability, performance, and results. Those require management and that, in turn, begins with the organization's mission.

As a rule, nonprofits are more money-conscious than business enterprises are. They talk and worry about money much of the time because it is so hard to raise and because they always have so much less of it than they need. But nonprofits do not base their strategy on money, nor do they make it the center of their plans, as so many corporate executives do. "The businesses I work with start their planning with financial returns," says one well-known CEO who sits on both business and nonprofit boards. "The nonprofits start with the performance of their mission."

Starting with the mission and its requirements may be the first lesson business can learn from successful nonprofits. It focuses the organization on action. It defines the specific strategies needed to attain the crucial goals. It creates a disciplined organization. It alone can prevent the most common degenerative disease of organizations, especially large ones: splintering their always limited resources on things that are "interesting" or look "profitable" rather than concentrating them on a very small number of productive efforts.

The best nonprofits devote a great deal of thought to defining their organization's mission. They avoid sweeping statements full of good intentions and focus, instead, on objectives that have clear-cut implications for the work their members perform—staff and volunteers both. The Salvation Army's goal, for example, is to turn society's rejects—alcoholics, criminals, derelicts—into citizens. The Girl Scouts help youngsters become confident, capable young women who respect themselves and other people. The Nature Conservancy preserves the diversity of nature's fauna and flora. Nonprofits also start with the environment, the community, the "customers" to be; they do not, as American businesses tend to do, start with the inside, that is, with the organization or with financial returns.

Willowcreek Community Church in South Barrington, Illinois, outside Chicago, has become the nation's largest church—some 13,000 parishioners. Yet it is barely 15 years old. Bill Hybels, in his early twenties when he founded the church, chose the community because it had relatively few churchgoers, though the population was growing fast and churches were plentiful. He went from door to door asking, "Why don't you go to church?" Then he designed a church to answer the potential customers' needs: for instance, it offers full services on Wednesday evenings because many working parents need Sunday to spend with their children. Moreover, Hybels continues to listen and react. The pastor's sermon is taped while it is being delivered and instantly reproduced so that parishioners can pick up a cassette when they leave the building because he was told again and again, "I need to listen when I drive home or drive to work so that I can build the message into my life." But he was also told: "The sermon always tells me to change my life but never how to do it." So now every one of Hybels's sermons ends with specific action recommendations.

A well-defined mission serves as a constant reminder of the need to look outside the organization not only for "customers" but also for measures of success. The temptation to content oneself with the "goodness of our cause"—and thus to substitute good intentions for results—always exists in nonprofit organizations. It is precisely because of this that the successful and performing nonprofits have learned to define clearly what changes *outside* the organization constitute "results" and to focus on them.

The experience of one large Catholic hospital chain in the Southwest shows how productive a clear sense of mission and a focus on results can be. Despite the sharp cuts in Medicare payments and hospital stays during the past eight years, this chain has increased revenues by 15% (thereby managing to break even) while greatly expanding its services and raising both patient-care and medical standards. It has done so because the nun who is its CEO understood that she and her staff are in the business of delivering health care (especially to the poor), not running hospitals.

As a result, when health care delivery began moving out of hospitals for medical rather than economic reasons about ten years ago, the chain promoted the trend instead of fighting it. It founded ambulatory surgery centers, rehabilitation centers, X-ray and lab networks, HMOs, and so on. The chain's motto was: "If it's in the patient's interest, we have to promote it; it's then our job to make it pay." Paradoxically, the policy has filled the chain's hospitals; the freestanding facilities are so popular they generate a steady stream of referrals.

This is, of course, not so different from the marketing strategy of successful Japanese companies. But it is very different indeed from the way most Western businesses think and operate. And the difference is that the Catholic nuns—and the Japanese—start with the mission rather than with their own rewards, and with what they have to make happen outside themselves, in the marketplace, to deserve a reward.

Finally, a clearly defined mission will foster innovative ideas and help others understand why they need to be implemented—however much they fly in the face of tradition. To illustrate, consider the Daisy Scouts, a program for five-year-olds which the Girl Scouts initiated a few years back. For 75 years, first grade had been the minimum age for entry into a Brownie troop, and many Girl Scout councils wanted to keep it that way. Others, however, looked at demographics and saw the growing numbers of working women with "latch key" kids. They also looked at the children and realized that they were far more sophisticated than their predecessors a generation ago (largely thanks to TV).

Today the Daisy Scouts are 100,000 strong and growing fast. It is by far the most successful of the many programs for preschoolers that have been started these last 20 years, and far more successful than any of the very expensive government programs. Moreover, it is so far the only program that has seen these critical demographic changes and children's exposure to long hours of TV viewing as an opportunity.

———————

Many nonprofits now have what is still the exception in business—a functioning board. They also have something even rarer: a CEO who is clearly accountable to the board and whose performance is reviewed annually by a board committee. And they have what is rarer still: a board whose performance is reviewed annually against preset performance objectives. Effective use of the board is thus a second area in which business can learn from the nonprofit sector.

In U.S. law, the board of directors is still considered the "managing" organ of the corporation. Management authors and scholars agree that strong boards are essential and have been writing to that effect for more than 20 years, beginning with Myles Mace's pioneering work.[1] Nevertheless, the top managements of our large companies have been whittling away at the directors' role, power, and independence for more than half a century. In every single business failure of a large company in the last few decades, the board was the last to realize that things were going wrong. To find a truly effective board, you are much better advised to look in the nonprofit sector than in our public corporations.

In part, this difference is a product of history. Traditionally, the board has run the shop in nonprofit organizations—or tried to. In fact, it is only because nonprofits have grown too big and complex to be run by part-time outsiders, meeting for three hours a month, that so many have shifted to professional management. The American Red Cross is probably the largest nongovernmental agency in the world and certainly one of the most complex. It is responsible for worldwide disaster relief; it runs thousands of blood banks as well as the bone and skin banks in hospitals; it conducts training in cardiac and respiratory rescue nationwide; and it gives first-aid courses in thousands of schools. Yet it did not have a paid chief executive until 1950, and its first professional CEO came only with the Reagan era.

But however common professional management becomes—and professional CEOs are now found in most nonprofits and all the bigger ones—nonprofit boards cannot, as a rule, be rendered impotent the way so many business boards have been. No matter how much nonprofit CEOs would welcome it—and quite a few surely would—nonprofit boards cannot become their rubber stamp. Money is one reason. Few directors in publicly held corporations are substantial shareholders, whereas directors on nonprofit boards very often contribute large sums themselves, and are expected to bring in donors as well. But also, nonprofit directors tend to have a personal commitment to the organization's cause. Few people sit on a church vestry or on a school board unless they deeply care about religion or education. Moreover, nonprofit board members typically have served as volunteers themselves for a good many years and are deeply knowledgeable about the organization, unlike outside directors in a business.

Precisely because the nonprofit board is so committed and active, its relationship with the CEO tends to be highly contentious and full of potential for friction. Nonprofit CEOs complain that their board "meddles." The directors, in turn, complain that management "usurps" the board's function. This has forced an increasing number of nonprofits to realize that neither board nor CEO is "the boss."

They are colleagues, working for the same goal but each having a different task. And they have learned that it is the CEO's responsibility to define the tasks of each, the board's and his or her own.

For example, a large electric co-op in the Pacific Northwest created ten board committees, one for every member. Each has a specific work assignment: community relations, electricity rates, personnel, service standards, and so on. Together with the coop's volunteer chairman and its paid CEO, each of these one-person committees defines its one-year and three-year objectives and the work needed to attain them, which usually requires five to eight days a year from the board member. The chairman reviews each member's work and performance every year, and a member whose performance is found wanting two years in a row cannot stand for reelection. In addition, the chairman, together with three other board members, annually reviews the performance of the entire board and of the CEO.

The key to making a board effective, as this example suggests, is not to talk about its function but to organize its work. More and more nonprofits are doing just that, among them half a dozen fair-sized liberal arts colleges, a leading theological seminary, and some large research hospitals and museums. Ironically, these approaches reinvent the way the first nonprofit board in America was set up 300 years ago: the Harvard University Board of Overseers. Each member is assigned as a "visitor" to one area in the university—the Medical School, the Astronomy Department, the investment of the endowment—and acts both as a source of knowledge to that area and as a critic of its performance. It is a common saying in American academia that Harvard has the only board that makes a difference.

The weakening of the large corporation's board would, many of us predicted (beginning with Myles Mace), weaken management rather than strengthen it. It would diffuse management's accountability for performance and results; and indeed, it is the rare big-company board that reviews the CEO's performance against preset business objectives. Weakening the board would also, we predicted, deprive top management of effective and credible support if it were attacked. These predictions have been borne out amply in the recent rash of hostile takeovers.

To restore management's ability to manage we will have to make boards effective again—and that should be considered a responsibility of the CEO. A few first steps have been taken. The audit committee in most companies now has a real rather than a make-believe job responsibility. A few companies—though so far almost no large ones—have a small board committee on succession and executive development, which regularly meets with senior executives to discuss their performance and their plans. But I know of no company so far where there are work plans for the board and any kind of review of the board's performance. And few do what the larger nonprofits now do routinely: put a new board member through systematic training.

Nonprofits used to say, "We don't pay volunteers so we cannot make demands upon them." Now they are more likely to say, "Volunteers must get far greater satisfaction from their accomplishments and make a greater contribution precisely because they do not get a paycheck." The steady transformation of the volunteer from well-meaning amateur to trained, professional, unpaid staff member is the most significant development in the nonprofit sector—as well as the one with the most far-reaching implications for tomorrow's businesses.

A Midwestern Catholic diocese may have come furthest in this process. It now has fewer than half the priests and nuns it had only 15 years ago. Yet it has greatly expanded its activities—in some cases, such as help for the homeless and for drug abusers, more than doubling them. It still has many traditional volunteers like the Altar Guild members who arrange flowers. But now it is also being served by some 2,000 part-time unpaid staff who run the Catholic charities, perform administrative jobs in parochial schools, and organize youth activities, college Newman Clubs, and even some retreats.

A similar change has taken place at the First Baptist Church in Richmond, Virginia, one of the largest and oldest churches in the Southern Baptist Convention. When Dr. Peter James Flamming took over five years ago, the church had been going downhill for many years, as is typical of old, inner-city churches. Today it again has 4,000 communicants and runs a dozen community outreach programs as well as a full complement of in-church ministries. The church has only nine paid full-time employees. But of its 4,000 communicants, 1,000 serve as unpaid staff.

This development is by no means confined to religious organizations. The American Heart Association has chapters in every city of any size throughout the country. Yet its paid staff is limited to those at national headquarters, with just a few traveling troubleshooters serving the field. Volunteers manage and staff the chapters, with full responsibility for community health education as well as fund raising.

These changes are, in part, a response to need. With close to half the adult population already serving as volunteers, their overall number is unlikely to grow. And with money always in short supply, the nonprofits cannot add paid staff. If they want to add to their activities—and needs are growing—they have to make volunteers more productive, have to give them more work and more responsibility. But the major impetus for the change in the volunteer's role has come from the volunteers themselves.

More and more volunteers are educated people in managerial or professional jobs—some preretirement men and women in their fifties, even more baby-boomers who are reaching their mid-thirties or forties. These people are not satisfied with being helpers. They are knowledge workers in the jobs in which they earn their living, and they want to be knowledge workers in the jobs in which they contribute to society—that is, their volunteer work. If nonprofit organizations want to attract and hold them, they have to put their competence and knowledge to work. They have to offer meaningful achievement.

Many nonprofits systematically recruit for such people. Seasoned volunteers are assigned to scan the newcomers—the new member in a church or synagogue, the neighbor who collects for the Red Cross— to find those with leadership talent and persuade them to try themselves in more demanding assignments. Then senior staff (either a full-timer on the payroll or a seasoned volunteer) interviews the newcomers to assess their strengths and place them accordingly. Volunteers may also be assigned both a mentor and a supervisor with whom they work out their performance goals. These advisers are two different people, as a rule, and both, ordinarily, volunteers themselves.

The Girl Scouts, which employs 730,000 volunteers and only 6,000 paid staff for 3½ million girl members, works this way. A volunteer typically starts by driving youngsters once a week to a meeting. Then a more seasoned volunteer draws her into other work—accompanying Girl Scouts selling cookies door-to-door, assisting a Brownie leader on a camping trip. Out of this step-by-step process evolve the volunteer boards of the local councils and, eventually, the Girl Scouts governing organ, the National Board. Each step, even the very first, has its own compulsory training program, usually conducted by a woman who is herself a volunteer. Each has specific performance standards and performance goals.

What do these unpaid staff people themselves demand? What makes them stay—and, of course, they can leave at any time. Their first and most important demand is that the nonprofit have a clear mission, one that drives everything the organization does. A senior vice president in a large regional bank has two small children. Yet she just took over as chair of the state chapter of Nature Conservancy, which finds, buys, and manages endangered natural ecologies. "I love my job," she said, when I asked her why she took on such heavy additional work, "and of course the bank has a creed. But it doesn't really know what it contributes. At Nature Conservancy, I know what I am here for."

The second thing this new breed requires, indeed demands, is training, training, and more training. And, in turn, the most effective way to motivate and hold veterans is to recognize their expertise and use them to train newcomers. Then these knowledge workers demand responsibility—above all, for thinking through and setting their own performance goals. They expect to be consulted and to participate in making decisions that affect their work and the work of the organization as a whole. And they expect opportunities for advancement, that is, a chance to take on more demanding assignments and more responsibility as their performance warrants. That is why a good many nonprofits have developed career ladders for their volunteers.

Supporting all this activity is accountability. Many of today's knowledge-worker volunteers insist on having their performance reviewed against preset objectives at least once a year. And increasingly, they expect their organizations to remove nonperformers by moving them to other assignments that better fit their capacities or by counseling them to leave. "It's worse than the Marine Corps boot camp," says the priest in charge of volunteers in the Midwestern diocese, "but we have 400 people on the waiting list." One large and growing Midwestern art museum requires of its volunteers—board members, fundraisers, docents, and the people who edit the museum's newsletter—that they set their goals each year, appraise themselves against these goals each year, and resign when they fail to meet their goals two years in a row. So does a fair-sized Jewish organization working on college campuses.

These volunteer professionals are still a minority, but a significant one—perhaps a tenth of the total volunteer population. And they are growing in numbers and, more important, in their impact on the nonprofit sector. Increasingly, nonprofits say what the minister in a large pastoral church says: "There is no laity in this church; there are only pastors, a few paid, most unpaid."

———————————

This move from nonprofit volunteer to unpaid professional may be the most important development in American society today. We hear a great deal about the decay and dissolution of family and community and about the loss of values. And, of course, there is reason for concern. But the nonprofits are generating a powerful countercurrent. They are forging new bonds of community, a new commitment to active citizenship, to social responsibility, to values. And surely what the nonprofit contributes to the volunteer is as important as what the volunteer contributes to the nonprofit. Indeed, it may be fully as important as the service, whether religious, educational, or welfare related, that the nonprofit provides in the community.

This development also carries a clear lesson for business. Managing the knowledge worker for productivity is the challenge ahead for American management. The nonprofits are showing us how to do that. It requires a clear mission, careful placement and continuous learning and teaching, management by objectives and self-control, high demands but corresponding responsibility, and accountability for performance and results.

There is also, however, a clear warning to American business in this transformation of volunteer work. The students in the program for senior and middle-level executives in which I teach work in a wide diversity of businesses: banks and insurance companies, large retail chains, aerospace and computer companies, real estate developers, and many others. But most of them also serve as volunteers in nonprofits—in a church, on the board of the college they graduated from, as scout leaders, with the YMCA or the Community Chest or the local symphony orchestra. When I ask them why they do it, far too many give the same answer: Because in my job there isn't much challenge, not enough achievement, not enough responsibility; and there is no mission, there is only expediency.

Originally published in July–August 1989. Reprint 89404

Note

1. A good example is Myles Mace, "The President and the Board of Directors," HBR, March–April 1972, p. 37.

An Interview with Desmond Tutu

Desmond Tutu *is often compared to Gandhi and Martin Luther King, Jr., as an iconic civil rights leader. But the South African archbishop emeritus demurs, joking that he won the 1984 Nobel Peace Prize because the committee was looking for an anti-apartheid figure with an easy-to-pronounce last name. "What I am is a good captain," Tutu said at the Skoll World Forum. "I utilize the talents of the people on the team, and when the team plays well, I get the kudos."* **Interviewed by Daniel McGinn**

HBR: *You aspired to become a physician, but instead became a teacher and then a clergyman. Did you ever consider a career in business?*

Tutu: No—I wouldn't have been good at that. When I have a little money, I spend it. And in the South Africa in which I grew up, you knew there was always going to be a ceiling; they wouldn't let a black person really prosper, and you'd be doing business under very serious constraints. Probably the only kind of businessperson a black person could be was a storekeeper, and the restrictions were so severe: You couldn't have your store in the white part of town; you were restricted in what you could do; you were restricted in terms of the customers you could serve. There was no way in which you could really become a serious rival to the main white shops. You were on totally unequal footing, and I don't think I'd have wanted to frustrate myself to that extent.

Overcoming apartheid took a remarkably long time. How did you find the patience?

For one thing, we didn't walk around feeling sorry for ourselves. We lived in a deprived setup, but we were not chafing at the bit. We were not sitting in the corner and weeping all the time—we were playing. We had fun. Life, to the extent that it could be, was fun. We also weren't as political as later generations were. But people can survive only so much repression—look at Libya, which lived that way for 40 years. Didn't they look around and see other parts of Africa gaining freedom? How come they allowed it? But it's an evolution. There's a lovely phrase in one of Paul's epistles: "In the fullness of time." Things are happening. There must have been people in Egypt who stood up for human rights, and it looked like they'd failed. But nothing is ever lost. The apparent failure is not in fact a failure. It's not something that dissipated into the ether.

Would apartheid have fallen faster in the age of Twitter and Facebook?

It might have. But actually people were able to communicate in spite of the Special Branch—a vicious security force that seemed to know everything about everything. Our community was riddled with informants. Someone who was suspected of being an informant would get a "burning necklace"—a tire around the neck that they'd light on fire. That's how they executed you. We always tried to step in, but there's no way to prove you're not an informant. But despite the imprisonments and the leaders who were exiled, people were not deterred. It just made them more determined. Dictators always think they are going to be there forever. Look at the number of African leaders who claimed they'd be president for life. [Big laugh.]

How did you build a coalition from such disparate groups?

I was just building on what other people were doing. During the struggle we were noble. People were altruistic—they weren't struggling against apartheid for what they could gain personally. Now, after apartheid, we're shocked to discover that people can be corrupt, that they can be working for their own self-advancement. But that wasn't the case during the struggle: It was really this incredible coalition. And it wasn't just in South Africa. You could go to almost any country in the world and you would find an anti-apartheid group. It was an extraordinary phenomenon.

How did you learn to use humor in leadership?

I have a family that likes pulling people's legs. They can be very funny. When you have to survive in that environment, you have to be pretty sharp yourself. In South Africa we became experts at conducting funerals, and people were angry and hurt over the mistreatment. But we also had this wonderful capacity to laugh. If we hadn't, we would have gone crazy. You know the saying—if we didn't laugh, we'd have to cry. I'm also aware that I was constantly being prayed for. There were times when I'd say something unrehearsed that surprised me, and I'd wonder, "Did I really say that? That was pretty smart." But it couldn't have just come spontaneously. Looking back, I have no doubt that some dear old ladies were kneeling down at Eucharist somewhere, praying to help the people struggling in South Africa. That prayer happened just at a time when I needed it. I believe that very firmly.

Originally published in July–August 2011. Reprint R1107S

Are You Solving the Right Problem?

by Dwayne Spradlin

"IF I WERE GIVEN ONE HOUR *to save the planet, I would spend 59 minutes defining the problem and one minute resolving it,"* Albert Einstein said.

Those were wise words, but from what I have observed, most organizations don't heed them when tackling innovation projects. Indeed, when developing new products, processes, or even businesses, most companies aren't sufficiently rigorous in defining the problems they're attempting to solve and articulating why those issues are important. Without that rigor, organizations miss opportunities, waste resources, and end up pursuing innovation initiatives that aren't aligned with their strategies. How many times have you seen a project go down one path only to realize in hindsight that it should have gone down another? How many times have you seen an innovation program deliver a seemingly breakthrough result only to find that it can't be implemented or it addresses the wrong problem? Many organizations need to become better at asking the right questions so that they tackle the right problems.

I offer here a process for defining problems that any organization can employ on its own. My firm, InnoCentive, has used it to help more than 100 corporations, government agencies, and foundations improve the quality and efficiency of their innovation efforts and, as a result, their overall performance. Through this process, which we call *challenge-driven innovation,* clients define and articulate their

35

business, technical, social, and policy issues and present them as challenges to a community of more than 250,000 solvers—scientists, engineers, and other experts who hail from 200 countries—on InnoCentive.com, our innovation marketplace. Successful solvers have earned awards of $5,000 to $1 million.

Since our launch, more than 10 years ago, we have managed more than 2,000 problems and solved more than half of them—a much higher proportion than most organizations achieve on their own. Indeed, our success rates have improved dramatically over the years (34% in 2006, 39% in 2009, and 57% in 2011), which is a function of the increasing quality of the questions we pose and of our solver community. Interestingly, even unsolved problems have been tremendously valuable to many clients, allowing them to cancel ill-fated programs much earlier than they otherwise would have and then redeploy their resources.

In our early years, we focused on highly specific technical problems, but we have since expanded, taking on everything from basic R&D and product development to the health and safety of astronauts to banking services in developing countries. We now know that the rigor with which a problem is defined is the most important factor in finding a suitable solution. But we've seen that most organizations are not proficient at articulating their problems clearly and concisely. Many have considerable difficulty even identifying which problems are crucial to their missions and strategies.

In fact, many clients have realized while working with us that they may not be tackling the right issues. Consider a company that engages InnoCentive to find a lubricant for its manufacturing machinery. This exchange ensues:

InnoCentive staffer: *"Why do you need the lubricant?"*
Client's engineer: *"Because we're now expecting our machinery to do things it was not designed to do, and it needs a particular lubricant to operate."*
InnoCentive staffer: *"Why don't you replace the machinery?"*
Client's engineer: *"Because no one makes equipment that exactly fits our needs."*

Idea in Brief

Eager to start working on solutions to innovation challenges, companies often don't spend enough time and resources on defining the problems they're trying to crack and establishing their importance to the organization. The results are missed opportunities, wasted resources, and initiatives that are out of sync with the strategy.

InnoCentive, an online innovation marketplace, has created a process that any organization can use to define problems and articulate their strategic importance. It involves four steps:

Clarifying the internal (company) or external (market or customer) need for a solution

Articulating the strategic importance of the solution to the firm

Researching how the firm and other organizations have already tried to solve the problem

Creating a clear and complete description of the problem

This raises a deeper question: Does the company need the lubricant, or does it need a new way to make its product? It could be that rethinking the manufacturing process would give the firm a new basis for competitive advantage. (Asking questions until you get to the root cause of a problem draws from the famous Five Whys problem-solving technique developed at Toyota and employed in Six Sigma.)

The example is like many we've seen: Someone in the bowels of the organization is assigned to fix a very specific, near-term problem. But because the firm doesn't employ a rigorous process for understanding the dimensions of the problem, leaders miss an opportunity to address underlying strategic issues. The situation is exacerbated by what Stefan Thomke and Donald Reinertsen have identified as the fallacy of "The sooner the project is started, the sooner it will be finished." (See "Six Myths of Product Development," HBR May 2012.) Organizational teams speed toward a solution, fearing that if they spend too much time defining the problem, their superiors will punish them for taking so long to get to the starting line.

Ironically, that approach is more likely to waste time and money and reduce the odds of success than one that strives at the outset to achieve an in-depth understanding of the problem

The problem-definition process

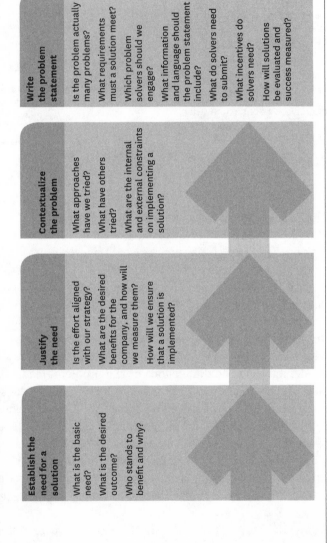

Establish the need for a solution

What is the basic need?

What is the desired outcome?

Who stands to benefit and why?

Justify the need

Is the effort aligned with our strategy?

What are the desired benefits for the company, and how will we measure them?

How will we ensure that a solution is implemented?

Contextualize the problem

What approaches have we tried?

What have others tried?

What are the internal and external constraints on implementing a solution?

Write the problem statement

Is the problem actually many problems?

What requirements must a solution meet?

Which problem solvers should we engage?

What information and language should the problem statement include?

What do solvers need to submit?

What incentives do solvers need?

How will solutions be evaluated and success measured?

and its importance to the firm. With this in mind, we developed a four-step process for defining and articulating problems, which we have honed with our clients. It consists of asking a series of questions and using the answers to create a thorough problem statement. This process is important for two reasons. First, it rallies the organization around a shared understanding of the problem, why the firm should tackle it, and the level of resources it should receive. Firms that don't engage in this process often allocate too few resources to solving major problems or too many to solving low-priority or wrongly defined ones. It's useful to assign a value to the solution: An organization will be more willing to devote considerable time and resources to an effort that is shown to represent a $100 million market opportunity than to an initiative whose value is much less or is unclear. Second, the process helps an organization cast the widest possible net for potential solutions, giving internal and external experts in disparate fields the information they need to crack the problem.

To illustrate how the process works, we'll describe an initiative to expand access to clean drinking water undertaken by the nonprofit EnterpriseWorks/VITA, a division of Relief International. EWV's mission is to foster economic growth and raise the standard of living in developing countries by expanding access to technologies and helping entrepreneurs build sustainable businesses.

The organization chose Jon Naugle, its technical director, as the initiative's "problem champion." Individuals in this role should have a deep understanding of the field or domain and be capable program administrators. Because problem champions may also be charged with implementing solutions, a proven leader with the authority, responsibility, and resources to see the project through can be invaluable in this role, particularly for a larger and more strategic undertaking. Naugle, an engineer with more than 25 years of agricultural and rural-development experience in East and West Africa and the Caribbean, fit the bill. He was supported by specialists who understood local market conditions, available materials, and other critical issues related to the delivery of drinking water.

Step 1: Establish the Need for a Solution

The purpose of this step is to articulate the problem in the simplest terms possible: "We are looking for X in order to achieve Z as measured by W." Such a statement, akin to an elevator pitch, is a call to arms that clarifies the importance of the issue and helps secure resources to address it. This initial framing answers three questions:

What is the basic need?

This is the essential problem, stated clearly and concisely. It is important at this stage to focus on the need that's at the heart of the problem instead of jumping to a solution. Defining the scope is also important. Clearly, looking for lubricant for a piece of machinery is different from seeking a radically new manufacturing process.

The basic need EWV identified was access to clean drinking water for the estimated 1.1 billion people in the world who lack it. This is a pressing issue even in areas that have plenty of rainfall, because the water is not effectively captured, stored, and distributed.

What is the desired outcome?

Answering this question requires understanding the perspectives of customers and other beneficiaries. (The Five Whys approach can be very helpful.) Again, avoid the temptation to favor a particular solution or approach. This question should be addressed qualitatively and quantitatively whenever possible. A high-level but specific goal, such as "improving fuel efficiency to 100 mpg by 2020," can be helpful at this stage.

In answering this question, Naugle and his team realized that the outcome had to be more than access to water; the access had to be convenient. Women and children in countries such as Uganda often must walk long distances to fetch water from valleys and then carry it uphill to their villages. The desired outcome EWV defined was to provide water for daily family needs without requiring enormous expenditures of time and energy.

Who stands to benefit and why?
Answering this question compels an organization to identify all potential customers and beneficiaries. It is at this stage that you understand whether, say, you are solving a lubricant problem for the engineer or for the head of manufacturing—whose definitions of success may vary considerably.

By pondering this question, EWV came to see that the benefits would accrue to individuals and families as well as to regions and countries. Women would spend less time walking to retrieve water, giving them more time for working in the field or in outside employment that would bring their families needed income. Children would be able to attend school. And over the longer term, regions and countries would benefit from the improved education and productivity of the population.

Step 2: Justify the Need

The purpose of answering the questions in this step is to explain why your organization should attempt to solve the problem.

Is the effort aligned with our strategy?
In other words, will satisfying the need serve the organization's strategic goals? It is not unusual for an organization to be working on problems that are no longer in sync with its strategy or mission. In that case, the effort (and perhaps the whole initiative) should be reconsidered.

In the case of EWV, simply improving access to clean drinking water wouldn't be enough; to fit the organization's mission, the solution should generate economic development and opportunities for local businesses. It needed to involve something that people would buy.

In addition, you should consider whether the problem fits with your firm's priorities. Since EWV's other projects included providing access to affordable products such as cookstoves and treadle pumps, the drinking water project was appropriate.

How Well-Defined Problems Lead to Breakthrough Solutions

The Subarctic Oil Problem

More than 20 years after the 1989 *Exxon Valdez* oil spill, cleanup teams operating in subarctic waters still struggled because oil became so viscous at low temperatures that it was difficult to pump from barges to onshore collection stations.

How the problem was defined

In its search for a solution, the Oil Spill Recovery Institute framed the problem as one of "materials viscosity" rather than "oil cleanup" and used language that was not specific to the petroleum industry. The goal was to attract novel suggestions from many fields.

The winner

A chemist in the cement industry was awarded $20,000 for proposing a modification of commercially available construction equipment that would vibrate the frozen oil, keeping it fluid.

The ALS Research Problem

By the late 2000s, researchers trying to develop a cure or treatment for amyotrophic lateral sclerosis (ALS, or Lou Gehrig's disease) had not made much progress. One major obstacle was the inability to detect and track the progression of the disease accurately and quickly. Because researchers could not know precisely what stage ALS sufferers had reached, they greatly increased the pool of participants in clinical trials and lengthened their studies, which drove up costs so much that few treatments were developed and evaluated.

How the problem was defined

Instead of framing its initiative as a search for a cure, Prize4Life, a nonprofit organization, focused on making ALS research feasible and effective.

What are the desired benefits for the company, and how will we measure them?

In for-profit companies, the desired benefit could be to reach a revenue target, attain a certain market share, or achieve specific

The solution it sought was a biomarker that would enable faster and more-accurate detection and measurement of the progression of the disease.

The winner

In 2011, a researcher from Beth Israel Hospital in Boston was paid $1 million for a noninvasive, painless, and low-cost approach, which detects ALS and assesses its progression by measuring changes in an electrical current traveling through muscle. This biomarker lowers the cost of ALS research by providing accurate and timely data that allow researchers to conduct shorter studies with fewer patients.

The Solar Flare Problem

In 2009 NASA decided it needed a better way to forecast solar flares in order to protect astronauts and satellites in space and power grids on Earth. The model it had been using for the past 30 years predicted whether radiation from a solar flare would reach Earth with only a four-hour lead time and no more than 50% accuracy.

How the problem was defined

NASA did not ask potential solvers simply to find a better way to predict solar flares; instead, it pitched the problem as a data challenge, calling on experts with analytic backgrounds to use one of the agency's greatest assets—30 years of space weather data—to develop a forecasting model. This data-driven approach not only invited solvers from various fields but also enabled NASA to provide instant feedback, using its archived data, on the accuracy of proposed models.

The winner

A semiretired radio-frequency engineer living in rural New Hampshire used data analysis and original predictive algorithms to develop a forecasting model that provided an eight-hour lead time and 85% accuracy. He was awarded $30,000 for this solution.

cycle-time improvements. EWV hoped to further its goal of being a recognized leader in helping the world's poor by transferring technology through the private sector. That benefit would be measured by market impact: How many families are paying for the solution?

How is it affecting their lives? Are sales and installation creating jobs? Given the potential benefits, EWV deemed the priority to be high.

How will we ensure that a solution is implemented?

Assume that a solution is found. Someone in the organization must be responsible for carrying it out—whether that means installing a new manufacturing technology, launching a new business, or commercializing a product innovation. That person could be the problem champion, but he or she could also be the manager of an existing division, a cross-functional team, or a new department.

At EWV, Jon Naugle was also put in charge of carrying out the solution. In addition to his technical background, Naugle had a track record of successfully implementing similar projects. For instance, he had served as EWV's country director in Niger, where he oversaw a component of a World Bank pilot project to promote small-scale private irrigation. His part of the project involved getting the private sector to manufacture treadle pumps and manually drill wells.

It is important at this stage to initiate a high-level conversation in the organization about the resources a solution might require. This can seem premature—after all, you're still defining the problem, and the field of possible solutions could be very large—but it's actually not too early to begin exploring what resources your organization is willing and able to devote to evaluating solutions and then implementing the best one. Even at the outset, you may have an inkling that implementing a solution will be much more expensive than others in the organization realize. In that case, it's important to communicate a rough estimate of the money and people that will be required and to make sure that the organization is willing to continue down this path. The result of such a discussion might be that some constraints on resourcing must be built into the problem statement. Early on in its drinking water project, EWV set a cap on how much it would devote to initial research and the testing of possible solutions.

Now that you have laid out the need for a solution and its importance to the organization, you must define the problem in detail.

This involves applying a rigorous method to ensure that you have captured all the information that someone—including people in fields far removed from your industry—might need to solve the problem.

Step 3: Contextualize the Problem

Examining past efforts to find a solution can save time and resources and generate highly innovative thinking. If the problem is industry-wide, it's crucial to understand why the market has failed to address it.

What approaches have we tried?

The aim here is to find solutions that might already exist in your organization and identify those that it has disproved. By answering this question, you can avoid reinventing the wheel or going down a dead end.

In previous efforts to expand access to clean water, EWV had offered products and services ranging from manually drilled wells for irrigation to filters for household water treatment. As with all its projects, EWV identified products that low-income consumers could afford and, if possible, that local entrepreneurs could manufacture or service. As Naugle and his team revisited those efforts, they realized that both solutions worked only if a water source, such as surface water or a shallow aquifer, was close to the household. As a result, they decided to focus on rainwater—which falls everywhere in the world to a greater or lesser extent—as a source that could reach many more people. More specifically, the team turned its attention to the concept of rainwater harvesting. "Rainwater is delivered directly to the end user," Naugle says. "It's as close as you can get to a piped water system without having a piped water supply."

What have others tried?

EWV's investigation of previous attempts at rainwater harvesting involved reviewing research on the topic, conducting five field studies, and surveying 20 countries to ask what technology was being used, what was and was not working, what prevented or encouraged the use of various solutions, how much the solutions cost, and what role government played.

"One of the key things we learned from the surveys," Naugle says, "was that once you have a hard roof—which many people do—to use as a collection surface, the most expensive thing is storage."

Here was the problem that needed to be solved. EWV found that existing solutions for storing rainwater, such as concrete tanks, were too expensive for low-income families in developing countries, so households were sharing storage tanks. But because no one took ownership of the communal facilities, they often fell into disrepair. Consequently, Naugle and his team homed in on the concept of a low-cost household rainwater-storage device.

Their research into prior solutions surfaced what seemed initially like a promising approach: storing rainwater in a 525-gallon jar that was almost as tall as an adult and three times as wide. In Thailand, they learned, 5 million of those jars had been deployed over five years. After further investigation, however, they found that the jars were made of cement, which was available in Thailand at a low price. More important, the country's good roads made it possible to manufacture the jars in one location and transport them in trucks around the country. That solution wouldn't work in areas that had neither cement nor high-quality roads. Indeed, through interviews with villagers in Uganda, EWV found that even empty polyethylene barrels large enough to hold only 50 gallons of water were difficult to carry along a path. It became clear that a viable storage solution had to be light enough to be carried some distance in areas without roads.

What are the internal and external constraints on implementing a solution?

Now that you have a better idea of what you want to accomplish, it's time to revisit the issue of resources and organizational commitment: Do you have the necessary support for soliciting and then evaluating possible solutions? Are you sure that you can obtain the money and the people to implement the most promising one?

Elements of a Successful Solution

ENTERPRISEWORKS/VITA SURVEYED POTENTIAL customers in Uganda to develop a list of must-have and nice-to-have elements for a product that would provide access to clean drinking water. The winning solution met all the criteria.

Must-Have

1. A price, including installation, of no more than $20

2. Storage capacity of at least 125 gallons

3. A weight light enough for one adult to carry a half mile on rough paths

4. Material that would prevent deterioration of water quality

5. An estimate of the cost of operating and maintaining the device over three years and a clear explanation of how to repair and replace components

6. A means, such as a filter, of removing gross organic matter from the incoming rain stream

7. A means, such as a tap or a pump, of extracting water without contaminating the contents of the unit

8. A method for completely draining the water and cleaning the system

Nice-to-Have

1. An aesthetically pleasing design

2. Additional functionality so that the unit could be used for multiple purposes

3. Features such as a modular design or salvageable parts that would add value to the device after its lifetime

External constraints are just as important to evaluate: Are there issues concerning patents or intellectual-property rights? Are there laws and regulations to be considered? Answering these questions may require consultation with various stakeholders and experts.

EWV's exploration of possible external constraints included examining government policies regarding rainwater storage. Naugle and his team found that the governments of Kenya, Tanzania, Uganda, and Vietnam supported the idea, but the strongest proponent was Uganda's minister of water and the environment, Maria

Mutagamba. Consequently, EWV decided to test the storage solution in Uganda.

Step 4: Write the Problem Statement

Now it's time to write a full description of the problem you're seeking to solve and the requirements the solution must meet. The problem statement, which captures all that the organization has learned through answering the questions in the previous steps, helps establish a consensus on what a viable solution would be and what resources would be required to achieve it.

A full, clear description also helps people both inside and outside the organization quickly grasp the issue. This is especially important because solutions to complex problems in an industry or discipline often come from experts in other fields (see "Getting Unusual Suspects to Solve R&D Puzzles," HBR May 2007). For example, the method for moving viscous oil from spills in Arctic and subarctic waters from collection barges to disposal tanks came from a chemist in the cement industry, who responded to the Oil Spill Recovery Institute's description of the problem in terms that were precise but not specific to the petroleum industry. Thus the institute was able to solve in a matter of months a challenge that had stumped petroleum engineers for years. (To read the institute's full problem statement, visit hbr.org/problem-statement1.)

Here are some questions that can help you develop a thorough problem statement:

Is the problem actually many problems?

The aim here is to drill down to root causes. Complex, seemingly insoluble issues are much more approachable when broken into discrete elements.

For EWV, this meant making it clear that the solution needed to be a storage product that individual households could afford, that was light enough to be easily transported on poor-quality roads or paths, and that could be easily maintained.

What requirements must a solution meet?

EWV conducted extensive on-the-ground surveys with potential customers in Uganda to identify the must-have versus the nice-to-have elements of a solution. (See the sidebar "Elements of a Successful Solution.") It didn't matter to EWV whether the solution was a new device or an adaptation of an existing one. Likewise, the solution didn't need to be one that could be mass-produced. That is, it could be something that local small-scale entrepreneurs could manufacture.

Experts in rainwater harvesting told Naugle and his team that their target price of $20 was unachievable, which meant that subsidies would be required. But a subsidized product was against EWV's strategy and philosophy.

Which problem solvers should we engage?

The dead end EWV hit in seeking a $20 solution from those experts led the organization to conclude that it needed to enlist as many experts outside the field as possible. That is when EWV decided to engage InnoCentive and its network of 250,000 solvers.

What information and language should the problem statement include?

To engage the largest number of solvers from the widest variety of fields, a problem statement must meet the twin goals of being extremely specific but not unnecessarily technical. It shouldn't contain industry or discipline jargon or presuppose knowledge of a particular field. It may (and probably should) include a summary of previous solution attempts and detailed requirements.

With those criteria in mind, Naugle and his team crafted a problem statement. (The following is the abstract; for the full problem statement, visit hbr.org/problem-statement2.)

EnterpriseWorks is seeking design ideas for a low-cost rainwater storage system that can be installed in households in developing countries. The solution is expected to facilitate access to clean water at a household level, addressing a problem that affects millions of people worldwide who are living in impoverished communities or rural areas where access to clean water is limited. Domestic rainwater harvesting is a proven technology that can be a valuable option for accessing and storing water year round. However, the high cost of available rainwater storage systems makes them well beyond the reach of low-income families to install in their homes.

A solution to this problem would not only provide convenient and affordable access to scarce water resources but would also allow families, particularly the women and children who are usually tasked with water collection, to spend less time walking distances to collect water and more time on activities that can bring in income and improve the quality of life.

What do solvers need to submit?

What information about the proposed solution does your organization need in order to invest in it? For example, would a well-founded hypothetical approach be sufficient, or is a full-blown prototype needed? EWV decided that a solver had to submit a written explanation of the solution and detailed drawings.

What incentives do solvers need?

The point of asking this question is to ensure that the right people are motivated to address the problem. For internal solvers, incentives can be written into job descriptions or offered as promotions and bonuses. For external solvers, the incentive might be a cash award. EWV offered to pay $15,000 to the solver who provided the best solution through the InnoCentive network.

How will solutions be evaluated and success measured?

Addressing this question forces a company to be explicit about how it will evaluate the solutions it receives. Clarity and transparency are crucial to arriving at viable solutions and to ensuring that the evaluation process is fair and rigorous. In some cases a "we'll know it when we see it" approach is reasonable—for example, when a company is looking for a new branding strategy. Most of the time, however, it is a sign that earlier steps in the process have not been approached with sufficient rigor.

EWV stipulated that it would evaluate solutions on their ability to meet the criteria of low cost, high storage capacity, low weight, and easy maintenance. It added that it would prefer designs that were modular (so that the unit would be easier to transport) and adaptable or salvageable or had multiple functions (so that owners could reuse the materials after the product's lifetime or sell them to others for various applications). The overarching goal was to keep costs low and to help poor families justify the purchase.

The Winner

Ultimately, the solution to EWV's rainwater-storage problem came from someone outside the field: a German inventor whose company specialized in the design of tourist submarines. The solution he proposed required no elaborate machinery; in fact, it had no pumps or moving parts. It was an established industrial technology that had not been applied to water storage: a plastic bag within a plastic bag with a tube at the top. The outer bag (made of less-expensive, woven polypropylene) provided the structure's strength, while the inner bag (made of more-expensive, linear low-density polyethylene) was impermeable and could hold 125 gallons of water. The two-bag approach allowed the inner bag to be thinner, reducing the price of the product, while the outer bag was strong enough to contain a ton and a half of water.

The structure folded into a packet the size of a briefcase and weighed about eight pounds. In short, the solution was affordable, commercially viable, could be easily transported to remote areas, and could be sold and installed by local entrepreneurs. (Retailers make from $4 to $8 per unit, depending on the volume they purchase. Installers of the gutters, downspout, and base earn about $6.)

EWV developed an initial version and tested it in Uganda, where the organization asked end users such questions as What do you think of its weight? Does it meet your needs? Even mundane issues like color came into play: The woven outer bags were white, which women pointed out would immediately look dirty. EWV modified the design on the basis of this input: For example, it changed the color of the device to brown, expanded its size to 350 gallons (while keeping the target price of no more than $20 per 125 gallons of water storage), altered its shape to make it more stable, and replaced the original siphon with an outlet tap.

After 14 months of field testing, EWV rolled out the commercial product in Uganda in March 2011. By the end of May 2012, 50 to 60 shops, village sales agents, and cooperatives were selling the product; more than 80 entrepreneurs had been trained to install it; and 1,418 units had been deployed in eight districts in southwestern Uganda.

EWV deems this a success at this stage in the rollout. It hopes to make the units available in 10 countries—and have tens or hundreds of thousands of units installed—within five years. Ultimately, it believes, millions of units will be in use for a variety of applications, including household drinking water, irrigation, and construction. Interestingly, the main obstacle to getting people to buy the device has been skepticism that something that comes in such a small package (the size of a typical five-gallon jerrican) can hold the equivalent of 70 jerricans. Believing that the remedy is to show villagers the installed product, EWV is currently testing various promotion and marketing programs.

As the EWV story illustrates, critically analyzing and clearly articulating a problem can yield highly innovative solutions. Organizations that apply these simple concepts and develop the skills and discipline to ask better questions and define their problems with more rigor can create strategic advantage, unlock truly groundbreaking innovation, and drive better business performance. Asking better questions delivers better results.

Originally published in September 2012. **Reprint** R1209F

An Interview with George Mitchell

George Mitchell *was a working-class boy from Maine who grew up to be the majority leader of the U.S. Senate and, as envoy to Northern Ireland, one of the most respected peace negotiators in the world.*
Interviewed by Alison Beard

HBR: *You've said that you use the same methods to resolve any dispute. What are they?*

Mitchell: First, there has to be a certain level of knowledge about the history and nature of the conflict. As an American working in Northern Ireland and the Middle East, I tried to fully inform myself by reading dozens of books about both conflicts. The second thing you need is a recognition that the people involved must own the resolution, because they're the ones who will live with the consequences. On the first day of formal negotiations in Northern Ireland, I told the assembled delegates, who represented 10 political parties and two governments, that I had not come there with an American plan, or a Clinton plan, or a Mitchell plan. I said, "Any agreement you are able to reach must be your own." That was very important in gaining their confidence. And nearly two years later, when I drafted the document that became the Good Friday Agreement, I was determined that every word in it be spoken or written by them. Third, you really must have deep reservoirs of patience and perseverance. I spent five years working on the peace process in Northern Ireland, chairing three separate sets of discussions. In the Middle East, I served two tours of duty, totaling about three years. The setbacks are many, and you can't get discouraged. You can't take the first or the second or the 10th no for a final answer. You just have to keep at it. Fourth, you have to gain the best possible understanding of the bottom line, or basic objectives, for each party. One of the most striking things about private disputes I mediate is how often people aren't really clear about that, which makes it very hard to reach a resolution. Finally, you have to be willing to take a risk when it's warranted. I decided to establish a firm deadline by which we would either succeed or fail in Northern Ireland, and it was a very close call. I was asked, "Why didn't you do that earlier?" But it wasn't just a matter of setting a deadline, it was timing, circumstance, the attitudes of the parties. All this, of course, is judgment.

With warring factions, how do you start a dialogue?

The challenge is not to get them to talk, because everybody will talk, but to get them to listen. This is true of humans everywhere: The receptors in our brain for information consistent with our prior beliefs are large and wide open, but the receptors for information that's contrary to them are much narrower. So we don't listen well to people we dislike or with whom we have a disagreement. It requires effort and discipline to get people to consider what the other side has to say. That's why these things take so long.

As an envoy and a senator, when you wanted to move people in a certain direction, how did you get them to listen to you?

What authority you have is derived largely from the respect and trust you're able to generate. I did the best I could by being open and fair. In the Senate you can't please everyone all the time. You're going to make decisions that anger some people. But shortly after I was elected majority leader, I met with Bob Dole, who was then the Republican leader. I said, "I know you've been around for many years and know much more than I do, but in my relatively short time, I've reached the conclusion that managing the Senate is impossible without some level of trust between the two leaders. So I'm here to tell you how I intend to behave toward you and ask you to behave toward me in the same way." I told him that I would never surprise him. I would give him as much notice as possible of every action I intended to take so that he could consider his response. I would never criticize him personally or try to embarrass him. I would always be available to him if he had a concern, question, or issue he wanted to raise. I would, to the extent humanly possible, always keep my word. And I could tell he was delighted. We shook hands, and never once since has a harsh word passed between us in public or in private. We disagreed on much legislation. We negotiated vigorously. But we succeeded in not making it personal and always trying to understand and accommodate each other.

Could you achieve the same bipartisan relationship today?

It was difficult even then, because there was an inherent conflict. As majority leader, I was in charge of all the operations of the Senate, and at the same time, I was the leader of the Senate Democratic caucus. So I had an obligation to the full Senate and an obligation to the party. But you have to keep your priorities straight. Your primary obligation is to the country and to the institution. That doesn't mean you surrender your principles. It means you understand that there are others who don't share them and who are entitled to express and advocate their views to the fullest extent permitted under the rules. But it is more difficult today for a whole variety of reasons. First, the divisions in Congress are a reflection of the divisions in our society. Many members of the public hold and advocate contradictory views. They say, "We want you to settle this without partisan dispute." But they also want it done in a manner consistent with their principles and beliefs. The challenge of political leadership is to reconcile those two requests. Second, technology has permitted the redrawing of congressional lines for the House so that the vast majority of seats are now held by one party, not by a particular candidate. So before the 2016 election you'll know the outcome—Republican or Democrat—even if you don't know who the person may be. Meanwhile, more representatives are running for and getting elected to the Senate and carrying with them the customs and mores of the House, which doesn't need as much tolerance and bipartisanship to function. Another factor is money. Our political system is drowning in it, and it's a truly corrupting influence. I travel all over America speaking, and I routinely ask audiences, "Does anyone believe that their member of Congress is more responsive to his or her constituents than to his or her donors?" In four years only one person has ever raised her hand—a woman in Washington. When, after the event, I asked her why, she said, "My husband is a congressman."

You obviously felt a very strong calling to serve your country in the public sector. Do you worry that the best and brightest are now moving into business, not government?

It's probably true that increasing numbers of young Americans are put off by the political process and not becoming involved to the extent that they once were. I think that's a loss for them and for our country. As I say in my book, I feel very lucky to be an American. My mother was an immigrant from Lebanon. My father was the orphan son of Irish immigrants. They had no education. My mother couldn't read or write English. They worked very hard at low-paying jobs all their lives, but they believed in the American dream. They had an exalted view of the value of an education, and I, their son, was lucky enough to get one. I've worked in law firms— I still work full time—and it's very rewarding to get the job done and be paid well. I served on corporate boards for diverse businesses— Disney, Federal Express, Staples—with people who had a passion for the work, which was interesting and enjoyable. But there just isn't any comparison between private rewards and rewards for public service. When I speak to graduates, I tell them that it's human nature to strive for status, wealth, possessions, recognition, but the more you succeed, the more you'll come to realize there's more to life than that, and nothing matches serving a cause larger than one's self-interest.

Early in your career you were described as mild-mannered and cerebral. How does someone who's not a natural extrovert become such a successful public figure?

When I ran for governor and lost, that was the description of me. I read and heard so much of it that I came to believe it. I thought I'd never again be involved in politics and certainly couldn't possibly win an election. But you learn from your mistakes and improve your performance. I don't know how many thousands of speeches I've given, but every time, I try to do the best I can and hope it's better than the one before. In politics, when you make a mistake, it's on the front page, so you become clearly aware of your faults and work at it more.

People also say you are extremely detail-oriented but never lose sight of the big picture. How do you manage that?

Both are essential. In Northern Ireland we had to come up with a document about which each leader could say, "This is good for us, for our specific constituency." At the same time, there had to be a broader vision of a society in which everyone was treated equally, regardless of background or religion—a society of tolerance and prosperity. So when I met with those politicians, I was very specific. I would say, "Look, you wanted ABC, and you've gotten it. The other side got DEF, even though you might not have wanted that. But the combination produces a society in which everybody can benefit." You need to merge intense and in-depth knowledge of the specific facts with that larger vision to get people to act positively.

You shocked everyone when you retired from the Senate. Why did you do it?

I decided after my first election, when I'd come from way behind in the polls to win, that I did not want to spend my entire life in the Senate. I felt extremely fortunate to be there, but this was not going to be my last act. Although I don't favor legal term limits, I wanted to limit myself. I was very much impressed by Senator Muskie, my mentor and friend, who left voluntarily to become secretary of state even though he'd been elected four times and probably could have been elected a couple more. When I decided to leave, I was reasonably certain I could have been reelected too. But I'd seen how the Senate consumed people, how serving and being reelected became not only the controlling but really the only factor in their lives. I wanted to serve, but I didn't want to lock myself into that position.

You then turned down a Supreme Court nomination to fight what would be a losing battle for health care reform. Have you ever had any regrets?

A couple of times, when I've read court decisions I didn't agree with, I've wished I'd been there to argue against them. The Citizens United case is one. I challenge anybody to read that decision and try to comprehend it. It is one of the least persuasive arguments I've ever read, based on wishful thinking, not the reality. To be clear, it didn't create the problem of excessive money in politics. But it was like putting gasoline on a fire. Very, very unfortunate. But the answer is, you do the best you can in life. You make decisions on the basis of information you have at the time. And once you make them, you go forward and don't spend your time agonizing over the past.

The envoy jobs you later took on were seen as missions impossible, but you tried anyway. Why?

We all get benefits from being citizens of this country, and with benefits come responsibilities. I anticipated the jobs would be very difficult, but I was asked to do them by the president of the United States. I also believe that there's no such thing as a conflict that can't be ended. Conflicts are created, conducted, and sustained by human beings. They can be ended by human beings. It takes a long time in some cases, but if I can get involved and help that happen earlier and save some lives in the process, that's a good thing.

You've led several investigations into institutional failures. How can integrity be spread through an organization where mistakes have been made?

The larger the organization, the more important it is to have a set of values and messages from the highest levels to people that they—and how they do their jobs—matter. Of course, every human is fallible. I've made so many mistakes in my life, it would take several hours of interviews to go over all of them. Our country has made many serious mistakes. But we acknowledge them. We try to correct them. We try to prevent them in the future. It's critical that people feel they're part of an entity that values good conduct. Leaders have to convey that success is defined not just by maximizing profit but by doing it in a manner consistent with the law, ethical guidelines, and personal and corporate integrity.

What do you consider your greatest accomplishment?

I think the answer to that should be left for others, but I take pride in a lot of things. Family is one. I've got three lovely children, and my brothers, my sister—we're all extremely close. I did some good things when I was in the Senate. We were fortunate in Northern Ireland, but really the political leaders there deserve the most credit. We weren't successful in the Middle East. I guess if you forced me to identify one thing, it would probably be my scholarship fund. I spend about a third of my time on that now. I was 16 when I graduated from high school—insecure, uncertain, had never really been anywhere or done anything, couldn't possibly have imagined what my life would be like. Meeting youngsters who reminded me of myself at that age sparked in me a desire to make it possible for every single child in Maine to have the same chance to go to college that I had.

Originally published in June 2015. Reprint R1506L

Enterprising Nonprofits

by J. Gregory Dees

Editor's Note: J. Gregory Dees wrote this article at a time when for-profit initiatives within nonprofits were becoming more common and controversial. Some of his examples now seem quaint (Save the Children selling neckties, for one), but Dees clearheadedly pushes past the details into the universal dilemma: Does commercial funding pull a nonprofit away from its social mission? And how does it change the character of a nonprofit's relationship with its beneficiaries? The framework Dees presents, the social enterprise spectrum, *is intended to help leaders of nonprofits understand and assess the options they face when exploring commercialization. It remains critical to all nonprofit organizations today.*

LAST AUGUST, THE AMERICAN MEDICAL ASSOCIATION backed out of an exclusive deal with Sunbeam Corporation, a manufacturer of such health-related products as thermometers and blood pressure monitors. The deal would have allowed Sunbeam to display an AMA seal of approval on some of its products—products that would then be packaged with AMA-sponsored health information. In return, Sunbeam would pay a royalty to the AMA on sales of the endorsed products.

The agreement sparked an outcry from the AMA's members and other observers who feared that it would compromise the integrity of the 150-year-old association. The reaction was so strong that the AMA's board of trustees was forced to rescind key terms of the deal just one week after announcing it. The revised policy specified that the association would not endorse products, accept royalties, or enter into exclusive arrangements with corporate partners. Sunbeam would be asked only to distribute the AMA's health information with its products and would pay the association only enough to cover the costs of producing the inserts. The AMA would not profit from the corporate use of its name.

The AMA's experience highlights how turbulent the new tide of commercialization in the nonprofit world can be. Faced with rising costs, more competition for fewer donations and grants, and increased rivalry from for-profit companies entering the social sector, nonprofits are turning to the for-profit world to leverage or replace their traditional sources of funding. In addition, leaders of nonprofits look to commercial funding in the belief that market-based revenues can be easier to grow and more resilient than philanthropic funding.

The drive to become more businesslike, however, holds many dangers for nonprofits. In the best of circumstances, nonprofits face operational and cultural challenges in the pursuit of commercial funding. In the worst, commercial operations can undercut an organization's social mission. To explore the new possibilities of commercialization and to avoid its perils, nonprofit leaders need to craft their strategies carefully. A framework—what I call the *social enterprise spectrum*—can help them understand and assess the options they face.

The Rising Tide of Commercialization

Nonprofit organizations have traditionally operated in the so-called social sector to solve or ameliorate such problems as hunger, homelessness, environmental pollution, drug abuse, and domestic violence. They have also provided certain basic social goods—such as education, the arts, and health care—that society believes the marketplace by itself will not adequately supply. Nonprofits have supplemented government activities, contributed ideas for new programs and other innovations, and functioned as vehicles for private citizens to pursue their own visions of the good society independent of government policy. Although some nonprofits have relied heavily on fees—especially those in the fields of health care and education—government grants

Idea in Brief

Faced with rising costs, more competition for fewer donations and grants, and increased rivalry from for-profit companies entering the social sector, nonprofits are turning to the commercial arena to leverage or replace their traditional sources of funding. The drive to become more business-like, however, holds many dangers for nonprofits. In the best of circumstances, nonprofits face operational and cultural challenges in the pursuit of commercial funding. In the worst, commercial operations can undercut an organization's social mission. To explore the new possibilities of commercialization and to avoid its perils, nonprofit leaders need to craft their strategies carefully. A framework—what the author calls the *social enterprise spectrum*—can help such leaders understand and assess their options.

Nonprofits first must identify potential sources of earned income; then they should set clear and realistic financial objectives. Commercial programs don't need to be profitable to be worthwhile. They can instead improve the efficiency and the effectiveness of organizations by reducing the need for donated funds; by providing a more reliable, diversified funding base; and by enhancing the quality of programs by instilling market discipline. In the end, commercial operations will not—and should not—drive out philanthropic initiatives. But thoughtful innovation in the social sector is essential if organizations are to leverage limited philanthropic resources.

and private donations have also accounted for a considerable portion of the funding that many nonprofits receive.

Recently, however, an increasing number of nonprofits have been seeking additional revenues by behaving more like for-profit organizations. Some are raising funds through auxiliary commercial enterprises. For example, Save the Children, an international development agency, sells a line of men's neckwear. Such ventures are for the most part bold, creative extensions of the old-fashioned bake sale or car wash: they get the word out about a nonprofit organization and its cause and, if successful, generate cash.

More dramatically, a number of nonprofits are beginning to commercialize the core programs through which they accomplish their missions; that is, they are looking for ways to make these programs rely less on donations and grants and more on fees and contracts. Some are accepting contracts from government agencies, for instance, to run social service programs, schools, and job-training programs for welfare recipients. Others are performing fee-based work for corporations or are charging beneficiaries directly for services that used to be free. For example, universities are engaging in contract research and are forming commercial partnerships to capitalize on the results of their noncontract research. Better Business Bureaus have explored charging a fee for reports on companies. Some nonprofits are even launching business enterprises to serve the objectives of their missions. For instance, San Francisco's Delancy Street Restaurant, run by the Delancy Street Foundation, is staffed by ex-convicts and former substance abusers who participate in Delancy's intensive self-help program and work in the restaurant as part of their rehabilitation. Finally, a few nonprofits, most notably hospitals and health maintenance organizations, are converting to for-profit status or are being acquired by for-profit companies.

Nonprofit leaders are scrambling to find commercial opportunities for a number of reasons. First, a new pro-business zeitgeist has made for-profit initiatives more acceptable. With the apparent triumph of capitalism worldwide, market forces are being widely celebrated. And with growing confidence in the power of competition and the profit motive to promote efficiency and innovation, many observers are suggesting that market discipline should exert more influence in the social sector—especially when those observers have fundamental doubts about the performance of social enterprises.

Second, many nonprofit leaders are looking to deliver social goods and services in ways that do not create dependency in their constituencies. Even many advocates for the poor or disadvantaged believe that institutional charity can undermine beneficiaries' self-esteem and create a sense of helplessness. As a result, some organizations are charging beneficiaries for at least a portion of the cost of services. Others seek to use business as a tool for helping people develop self-reliance and build marketable capabilities. One important study of nonprofit businesses that help the homeless and other disadvantaged groups become self-sufficient was recently published by Jed Emerson of the Roberts Foundation (now called the Roberts Enterprise Development Fund and originally created by George Roberts of the LBO firm, Kholberg, Kravis, and Roberts). The study documents a host of job-creating nonprofit businesses—such as bakeries, ice cream shops, and greeting-card and silk-screened T-shirt stores—all in the San Francisco Bay Area.

Third, nonprofit leaders are searching for the holy grail of financial sustainability. They view earned-income-generating activities as more reliable funding sources than donations and grants. Many of them now consider extensive dependency on donors as a sign of weakness and vulnerability. Self-funding is the new mantra. At a minimum, organizations seek a diversity of funding sources to provide a cushion in case one source declines or disappears. Commercial funding is particularly attractive because it is potentially unrestricted: owners of a commercial enterprise can use excess revenues for whatever purposes they like, whereas the use of grants and donations to nonprofits is often restricted to particular projects and purposes. Furthermore, commercial markets are potentially huge.

Fourth, the sources of funds available to nonprofits are shifting to favor more commercial approaches. Competition for philanthropic dollars is intense, but money is becoming available for operating on a more commercial basis. Consider the following changes: Today few foundations want to provide ongoing funding—even to highly successful projects. Most choose to limit their funding to short periods in an effort to press grantees to become increasingly self-sufficient. At the same time, government agencies are shifting from providing services themselves to contracting with independent nonprofit and for-profit organizations. Such contracting creates opportunities, but government grant programs are being cut or threatened. Finally, corporations are thinking more strategically about philanthropy. They are no longer deciding where their grant dollars will go solely on the merits of the programs they will fund but on the value they will derive from the relationship with a particular nonprofit. Some corporations are exploring the benefits of direct business relationships with nonprofits, and others have started paying for social services as an employee benefit—again creating new commercial opportunities in the social sector.

Fifth, competitive forces are leading nonprofit managers to consider commercial alternatives to traditional sources of funding. New for-profit companies have made considerable headway in health care and are beginning to enter other social services—such as running orphanages, managing charter schools, and providing welfare-to-work programs. As for-profit companies enter an industry and some nonprofits start experimenting with commercial operations, other nonprofits feel pressured to follow the lead of their competitors that are turning to commercial sources of revenue. For instance, many nonprofit hospitals mimic the management styles and methods of their for-profit counterparts. Similarly, if some major universities subsidize their operations by commercializing research, others will do the same—if only to maintain a competitive cost structure. Once commercialization in a social-sector industry begins, many nonprofits jump on the bandwagon—even if questions remain about how successful those operations ultimately will be.

Navigating Dangerous Currents

Market-based funding approaches do have an important role to play in the social sector. If those social programs that are able to generate their own income in fact do so, philanthropic dollars can be allocated to activities that truly need to be subsidized. But embracing commercial opportunities can be risky. The often perilous currents of commercialization in the social sector must be navigated with care. There are a number of dangers that nonprofit leaders should be aware of.

Like the proverbial tail wagging the dog, new sources of revenue can pull an organization away from its original social mission. Consider the YMCA. The association today generates substantial revenues by operating health-and-fitness facilities for middle-class families, but critics charge that the YMCA has lost sight of its mission to promote the "spiritual, mental, and social condition of young men." Similarly, a former board member of a major dance company resigned because he felt the company had neglected its artistic mission and had become too commercial by performing popular pieces to generate revenue. Of course, changing a mission in order to ensure the survival of a worthwhile organization may be justifiable. But nonprofits should be aware that by seizing market opportunities, they may be drawn incrementally and unintentionally into new arenas far from their original focus.

Nonprofit leaders should also recognize that creating a sustainable and profitable business is not easy. Market discipline can be harsh. Some studies indicate that more than 70% of new businesses fail within eight years of their inception. Substantial profits, although not impossible to achieve, are hard to come by. In perfectly competitive markets, companies make only enough to cover costs and to compensate capital providers adequately. Running a profitable business requires skill, luck, and flexibility. Nonprofits may have some advantages when competing in commercial markets. Those advantages include their tax status and their ability to capitalize on volunteer labor, to attract in-kind donations and supplier discounts, and to use philanthropic money to help cover start-up costs and capital investments. But those advantages alone will not ensure profitability.

Many nonprofits simply do not have the business-specific organizational skills, managerial capacity, and credibility to succeed in commercial markets. And building new organizational capabilities can be costly and difficult. Hiring people with business skills and market focus is not enough. An organization must be receptive to and supportive of new activities; it also must be able to integrate the skills and values of the new staff. Many MBAs who go to work in nonprofit organizations find themselves ostracized by their colleagues. One business school graduate and former brand manager at a major corporation, who now heads a division of a nonprofit devoted to environmental protection, spent several years overcoming the skepticism of core staff members. In that organization, scientific credentials and a demonstrated commitment to the environment were signs of prestige; business skills were suspect. The division head's staff feared that he would focus on the bottom line to the exclusion of the mission.

Indeed, the culture of commerce can conflict with that of the social sector in several ways. Many who work in nonprofits are uncomfortable with the style of operations common to for-profit organizations. Consider the conflicts that occurred at a major non-governmental organization operating in a developing country. On one side were the social workers who were committed to helping their poverty-stricken clientele. On the other side were the loan officers in the newly formed, self-sustaining microloan operation, which helps some of the same clients start small businesses. When the loan officers had to demand payments from a client, the social workers objected. They found this kind of businesslike behavior offensive; it ran counter to their sense of compassion. Although nonprofits have become more accepting of business in general, some nonprofit managers still bristle at the use of business language. Even the word *customer* can put people off. The leader of one community-based arts organization, uncomfortable with the idea of being customer driven, contends that her mission is to provide a forum for avant-garde African-American playwrights, not to cater to the tastes of a local audience. And she is far from unique. Social workers, curators, educators, doctors, nurses, artists, scientists, and other professionals who staff nonprofits may balk when they are expected to adapt more to businesslike methods of operation.

Commercialization can also undermine the role a nonprofit organization plays in its community. Community-based nonprofits often serve as outlets for citizens to act on their philanthropic impulses—to join voluntarily in efforts to improve the conditions of their community. The executive director of a major food bank believes that the mission of his organization is not only to supply food for the needy but also to provide opportunities for people from all walks of life to volunteer, to serve the poor, and to interact with one another. Volunteers may not be so ready to contribute their time to for-profit programs. Although commercialization need not drive out philanthropic activities, the two impulses can be difficult to balance.

When nonprofits become more businesslike, they may run afoul of public values and meet with political resistance. For instance, the Red Cross blood-bank system has come under attack recently for its attempt to create a national system of distribution, its allegedly aggressive pursuit of donors, and its alleged failure to serve hospitals that favor other blood providers. Of course, the Red Cross has defended itself against those charges, but the point is that nonprofits are not expected to behave like businesses. When they do, critics are ready to pounce.

Nonprofits that undertake commercial initiatives also face resistance from for-profit competitors. Nonprofits are perceived to have the unfair advantages of tax breaks and lower costs for labor, capital, and supplies. Cross-sector competition exists in industries from day care to publishing to gift catalogs. For-profit providers of adult education services complain about nonprofit rivals. Local retailers don't like competing with university-owned stores that sell not only textbooks but also clothing, computers, records—items that have little to do with a school's educational mission. If the competition continues to heat up, for-profit rivals will step up the pressure for a reconsideration of the tax exemptions offered to nonprofits.

Charting a Favorable Course

Despite the risks of commercialization, nonprofit leaders can chart a favorable course through commercial waters in their search for ways both to reduce their organizations' dependence on grants and to enhance their mission-related performance. The challenge is to find a financial structure that reinforces the organization's mission, uses scarce resources efficiently, is responsive to changes, and is practically achievable.

To begin, nonprofit leaders must understand the full range of available options. A social enterprise is commercial to the extent that it operates like a business in how it acquires its resources and distributes its goods and services. The more commercial an organization, the less it relies on philanthropy. Few social enterprises can or should be purely philanthropic or purely commercial; most should combine commercial and philanthropic elements in a productive balance. Many already do. (See the exhibit "The social enterprise spectrum," which shows the range of commercialization in terms of a nonprofit's relationships with its key stakeholders.)

The social enterprise spectrum

Motives, methods, and goals	Purely philanthropic →		Purely commercial
	Appeal to goodwill	Mixed motives	Appeal to self-interest
	Mission driven	Mission and market driven	Market driven
	Social value	Social and economic value	Economic value

Key stakeholders	Purely philanthropic		Purely commercial
Beneficiaries	Pay nothing	Subsidized rates, or mix of full payers and those who pay nothing	Market-rate prices
Capital	Donations and grants	Below-market capital, or mix of donations and market-rate capital	Market-rate capital
Workforces	Volunteers	Below-market wages, or mix of volunteers and fully paid staff	Market-rate compensation
Suppliers	Make in-kind donations	Special discounts, or mix of in-kind and full-price donations	Market-rate prices

For instance, colleges and universities charge a tuition that does not cover operating costs because such institutions can draw on alumni donations, research grants, and income from endowments. Some nonprofits cross-subsidize one program or client group with another. Many day care centers use a sliding fee scale so that wealthier families subsidize poorer ones. Ballet companies often use profits from holiday performances of the *Nutcracker* to support artistically important but unprofitable productions. Still other nonprofits obtain funding from third-party payers, such as governments and corporations. Health care providers commonly receive the bulk of their revenues from public and private insurance plans. Social service providers can contract with state government agencies to provide their services to state residents.

As they evaluate their organizations' potential to operate at the commercial end of the spectrum, nonprofit leaders should begin by identifying all potential commercial sources of revenue. Potential paying customers include the organization's intended beneficiaries, third parties with a vested interest in the mission, and others for whom the organization can create value.

Earned income from intended beneficiaries

In an ideal world, social enterprises would receive funding and attract resources only when they produced their intended social impact—such as alleviating poverty in a given area, reducing drug abuse, delivering high-quality education, or conserving natural resources. The best strategy in this ideal world would be to ask the intended beneficiaries to pay full cost for services. After all, the beneficiary would be in a prime position to determine if the value created was sufficiently high to justify the costs of creating it. In the real world, however, this approach works only for nonprofits that are in the business of serving a clearly defined and well-informed consumer who is able to pay. Membership organizations are one example; their beneficiaries, or members, pay for services through membership fees.

Few nonprofits will be able to reduce their missions to that kind of formula. The intended beneficiaries of a social enterprise are rarely well-informed, viable, or appropriate payers. In some instances, it isn't even clear who the intended beneficiaries are. Who is the intended beneficiary of a project to save the whales from extinction? The whales? The general public? Future generations? In many social enterprises, the intended beneficiary is unable to pay anything close to the cost of the services delivered. For instance, if development agencies such as CARE, Save the Children, and Oxfam—agencies that serve poor, distressed communities—relied exclusively on fees charged to residents, they would be able to operate only in relatively wealthy communities.

In other instances, beneficiaries may not be sufficiently knowledgeable to make an informed purchase decision. Or they may not fully appreciate the value of the service being offered. For example, abusive spouses who recognize that they have a problem but underestimate its severity might not realize the benefit of counseling to themselves and to their families until after they have gone through a program. If full payment were required, they might not undergo counseling at all. Because collective goods are often at stake in the work of nonprofits, society might lose in such an exchange as well. For example, society benefits from the drop in crime rates that occurs if addicts are treated in rehabilitation programs; but if addicts were required to pay the full cost of the program, few would join.

Finally, requiring intended beneficiaries to pay may be inappropriate, even when it is feasible. Commercialization can often change the character of a nonprofit's relationship with its beneficiaries. Imagine Amnesty International charging a fee to the political prisoners who are released as a result of its activities or the Red Cross charging disaster victims for relief services. If Big Brothers and Big Sisters charged children or their families for a mentor's time, wouldn't the child suspect that the mentor was there simply for the pay, and wouldn't that suspicion undermine the relationship?

To understand the full range of commercial options, nonprofit leaders should evaluate potential revenues for all beneficiary groups, services, and products. Assumptions about the viability and appropriateness of charging for services also should be explored and questioned. For instance, should a group that serves people with disabilities assume that its constituency could not or should not pay for any of the services it provides? In fact, it can be demeaning to treat people with disabilities as charity cases. Asking for at least some payment can give beneficiaries a sense of responsibility and enhance their commitment to the treatment. In programs requiring the active participation of beneficiaries, pricing serves to screen out those who are not sufficiently serious about the program. If the intended beneficiaries vary in their ability to pay, nonprofit leaders should examine the feasibility and desirability of cross-subsidization and discounted fees. The organization could use sliding fee scales, scholarships, special discounts, and other devices to allow access to people of lesser means. It could also opt for deferred payments along the lines of student loans for higher education. A more radical alternative to deferred payments would be to encourage pre-payment or group payment using membership fees or an insurance scheme. Some colleges already offer to guarantee tuition rates many years into the future if parents pay tuition in advance.

Earned income from third-party payers with a vested interest

Faced with the difficulties of charging intended beneficiaries for services rendered, social enterprises often need to search for next-best solutions. To that end, nonprofits can look to third-party funding sources. The most likely direct payers are government agencies and corporations that have a vested interest in an intended beneficiary group or in the enterprise's mission. The government's role as a source of revenue for certain nonprofit organizations is widely recognized. It has a vested interest in collective goods and in the welfare of the poor. Corporations play a similar role when they subsidize such employee benefits as health care, day care, elder care, family counseling, and alcohol and drug rehabilitation.

Third-party payment can take many forms. The payers can issue vouchers to be used at the discretion of the beneficiary, can reimburse for services chosen by beneficiaries, or can contract directly for service delivery. Contracting itself can range from cost plus to flat rates per capita. In many cases, the beneficiaries share some of the costs through co-payments and deductibles. This approach appealed to the founders of GuateSalud, a health maintenance organization for the rural working poor in Guatemala. After struggling to raise donations for their work, the founders decided to market their health services to the owners of small coffee plantations who employ poor migrant workers during the harvest season. The owners paid a monthly fee for the service, and workers paid token fees for visits to the health facility and for pharmaceuticals. The arrangement was a success: the owners got a healthier workforce, and the workers gained access to medical care and health education that otherwise would not have been available to them.

Nonprofit leaders considering this option need to ask how closely the interests of third-party payers align with the organization's mission. If the interests diverge from the mission now or in the future, how can the mission be protected? The challenge nonprofit leaders face, then, is to find third parties whose interests fit the enterprise's mission and to maximize that alignment. They need to conduct a thorough, fact-based assessment to determine the impact of potential arrangements on the mission. For instance, if it is important for GuateSalud to improve the overall health of poor native Guatemalans, is contracting with the plantation owners, who have access to many of those workers only during harvest, enough? The answer to that question depends in large part on whether a brief health intervention at harvest time makes a significant difference in health outcomes. The question also must be weighed in the context of alternatives: if funding isn't available for a more substantial intervention, such as placing clinics in remote regions or having health providers travel extensively, contracting with the owners may be better than nothing.

As they conduct their assessment, nonprofit leaders should also consider such practical matters as the costs of negotiating contracts and managing the ongoing relationship with a third-party payer. In some cases, particularly in the case of government contracting, the nonprofit can incur considerable incremental administrative costs.

Finally, nonprofit leaders should evaluate how reliable the revenue stream will be over time. It can be risky for a nonprofit to have just one or a few major payers because a canceled contract would be a major blow to the organization. For instance, Leeway, a nursing home for people with AIDS, depends heavily on Connecticut Medicaid reimbursements. A change in state policy could prevent Leeway from fulfilling its mission. A single funding source may be the best available to an organization such as Leeway, but leaders need to consider the associated risks. Changing funding sources can be quite disruptive and can require a great deal of management time. Yet, some disruptions may be necessary, considering that the alternative—philanthropic fund-raising—is also very time consuming and uncertain.

Earned income from others
In addition to obtaining direct payments for mission-related services, nonprofits can receive indirect sources of earned income from third parties. One common form of indirect commercial support is advertising. Corporations may pay for the right to promote their products to a nonprofit's target market. For instance, companies that make baby products might sponsor an educational program for mothers of low-birth-weight infants. So-called cause-related marketing, in which a company uses its support of a nonprofit cause in its promotions, is an extension of this idea. In addition, nonprofits can use their name recognition to *co-brand* products, such as pain relievers endorsed by the Arthritis Foundation. Businesses and individuals also can indirectly support social enterprises by purchasing goods and services. Local hotels and hospitals might contract for services from a commercial laundry operated by a homeless shelter to provide job training and income to residents. In such a case, the third parties are paying the shelter not to provide training for homeless people but to provide laundry services; in other words, they are paying the shelter indirectly to serve its primary constituency.

Finding indirect sources of revenue often requires creativity. Nonprofit leaders should ask themselves how their organizations could create value for someone who would pay. Because this source of earned income is the one least directly related to mission performance, it can risk pulling the organization off course by diverting valuable management resources away from activities related to the organization's core mission. As a result, leaders need to be particularly careful to question the appropriateness of this kind of financial relationship. Will the demands of running a competitive commercial laundry create pressure to employ only shelter residents who already have good job skills, those least in need of training? When corporations with vested interests pay for research, will universities shift resources from basic science to more applied areas? Will they become scientific advocates for the interests of their paying clients?

Choosing the Right Vessel

Once nonprofits identify potential sources of earned income, they should set clear and realistic financial objectives. Commercial programs don't need to be profitable to be worthwhile. They can improve the efficiency and effectiveness of the organization by reducing the need for donated funds, by providing a more reliable, diversified funding base, or by enhancing the quality of programs by instilling market discipline. Following are the possible financial approaches that a nonprofit might adopt. They move roughly from left to right on the social enterprise spectrum.

Full philanthropic support

After reviewing their options, the leaders of a nonprofit might decide that no potential sources of earned income are appealing, given the organization's mission and values. They must then decide on the right mixture of philanthropic sources: cash donations, in-kind donations, and volunteer labor. Very few nonprofits will be staffed solely by volunteers and will acquire all their equipment, facilities, and supplies as in-kind donations. For most organizations, cash donations provide a way to adopt more commercial labor and purchasing practices. For instance, a mentoring program for disadvantaged youth could have a paid staff, volunteer adult mentors, some in-kind donations, and a variety of cash operating expenses, and could rely exclusively on grants and donations to cover all out-of-pocket costs. Many new and small social-service nonprofits operate this way, with negligible or no earned income.

Partial self-sufficiency

Other nonprofits might conclude that the sources of earned income available to them will cover only part of their necessary operating expenses, even when taking into account potential in-kind donations and volunteer labor. They will need cash donations to pay for some out-of-pocket operating expenses, as well as for startup costs and capital investments. Most institutions of higher education operate this way. Tuition covers only a portion of total costs; donors subsidize the rest. The difficulty such organizations face is determining the right level of subsidy. To determine that level, they must assess not only potential commercial and philanthropic revenues but also competitive dynamics, values, and mission-related objectives.

For example, Berea College in Berea, Kentucky, targets financially needy Appalachian students and charges no tuition. All students work, but the college covers its costs largely through income from a sizable endowment and annual giving. In contrast, Vermont's Bennington College decided from the start that it did not want to be beholden to donors who might interfere with its mission. (Bennington was founded as an experimental college for women and emphasized individualized, nontraditional courses of study.) The college did not run annual fund-raising campaigns and built a negligible endowment. Instead, it charged a high tuition; in fact, its tuition was frequently one of the highest in the nation.

Both schools have long delivered high-quality education. So which model is best? The answer to that question depends both on how well the model serves the institution's mission and on the model's feasibility for sustaining its institution. Bennington's model would not have worked for Berea's mission serving the Appalachian poor. For a time in the 1980s and early 1990s, it did not work very well for Bennington's mission either. High costs and competition for students made the pay-as-you-go model difficult to maintain. The college recently restructured and has launched a capital campaign to build an endowment, but Bennington will not need an endowment as large as Berea's.

Cash flow self-sufficiency

Many nonprofit social enterprises want commercial revenues but not market-based costs. They use earned income to cover out-of-pocket operating expenses, but the costs they incur are lower than market rates because of their ready access to philanthropic investment capital (such as grants and below-market program-related investments made by foundations), volunteers (or below-market wages), and in-kind donations (or discounts). Such organizations are technically self-funding and may even generate excess cash to cover the costs of strapped mission-related activities, but they still depend on noncash philanthropic subsidies.

Help the World See (HTWS) and the new permanent eye-care clinics it has established in developing countries illustrate how this model works. When HTWS began, it sent volunteer doctors with donated glasses to developing countries to set up temporary clinics. Then five years ago, the organization embarked on a new strategy. It would establish permanent clinics, offering affordable ongoing eye care, that would operate self-sufficiently on a cash-flow basis. Start-up capital would be donated; in-kind space would be provided by governments or sympathetic nongovernmental organizations; materials to produce glasses would be acquired at a discount from willing suppliers; and staff training would be covered by grants. But the organization would pay the staff and cover out-of-pocket operating expenses by charging a small fee for glasses. The new strategy demanded a trade-off: the stand-alone clinics would not be able to serve—at least not initially—the very poorest residents, who could not afford even the small fee for glasses. (It was hoped that one day the clinics would be able to generate a "profit" to pay for services for the very poor.) But the clinics could still serve many who were not able to find or afford glasses any other way.

Operating expense self-sufficiency

Nonprofits may be able to have earned income cover all operating expenses, even if those expenses are at market rates. They might obtain donations or below-market loans to cover some start-up expenses and capital expenditures, but after that, the operation would stand on its own without relying on additional philanthropy of any kind, including volunteer and in-kind donations. Few social ventures launched by nonprofits can aspire to this degree of independence from philanthropic support when it comes to operations. One example of a nonprofit organization that has adopted this model is the Kentucky Highlands Investment Corporation. It began with nearly $15 million in grants from the federal government to use as venture capital to stimulate economic development in several distressed counties in southeastern Kentucky. Using returns from its investments, the corporation has been able to cover its operating costs for the venture fund and to make new investments—in the process preserving the value of the fund.

Even when operating self-sufficiency is the goal, most new ventures will need some form of cash subsidy during the start-up period. But nonprofit leaders must decide how long to subsidize the venture. Cutting one's losses in mission-related operations can be difficult: when a new program cannot stand on its own, a nonprofit may have to decide whether to continue the program even though it will need to be subsidized. Shutting down a program may have political costs or an unfortunate impact on an organization's mission. For instance, the Bangladesh Rural Advancement Committee (BRAC) created a silk industry from scratch in Bangladesh to employ women and the landless poor. BRAC intended for all parts of the industry's value chain—from growing mulberry trees to selling the products made with BRAC silk—to operate self-sufficiently. But the silk-reeling plants were very inefficient, in large part because of the inherently poor quality of the cocoons that were bred to grow in Bangladesh. To pay its workers a living wage, BRAC had to accept losses on this stage in the production process. Shutting down the plants would have crippled the entire silk project, hurting thousands of workers and strengthening the hand of BRAC's fundamentalist political opponents. BRAC intends to work to make the plants profitable, but it will be difficult to pull the plug on this operation even if profitability is never achieved.

Full-scale commercialization

When an organization is fully commercial, revenue covers all costs at market rates, including the market cost of capital, without a hint of philanthropic subsidy even for start-up expenses. The organization repays start-up capital at a market rate of return and is sufficiently profitable to attract new investment capital for expansion. Few nonprofits can achieve full-scale commercialization. Because nonprofits cannot accept equity investments and it is difficult to be financed totally with debt, such organizations often are structured as, or convert to, for-profit enterprises.

Nonprofits that are this strongly committed to commercialization—and to their independence from philanthropic subsidies—face a challenging balancing act. On the one hand, they will need to act like businesses by preserving their flexibility and by being willing to cut losses and search for new sources of revenue. On the other hand, they will have to do so within the constraints of their mission. Absent a philanthropic cushion and a commitment to philanthropic supporters, nonprofit leaders will need to keep the enterprise's mission in mind when reacting to business pressures.

Mixed enterprises

Finally, it should be noted that many social enterprises are actually multi-unit operations that run programs with different financial objectives and funding structures. A major museum might have both a profitable catalog business and a highly subsidized research-and-acquisition operation. The Nature Conservancy established a for-profit company, the Eastern Shore Sustainable Development Corporation, in order to generate profits and create jobs while protecting the environment. The conservancy has partnered with for-profit companies such as Georgia Pacific to find profitable ways to conserve natural habitats, and it offers ecological travel programs for a fee to its members. Yet many of its core conservation activities still rely heavily on donations.

Other multi-unit social enterprises are for-profit organizations with nonprofit affiliates. Shorebank Corporation, for instance, is a development bank with a social mission. It has commercial-banking and real estate operations, as well as an affiliate nonprofit community-development corporation that is dependent on grants. The corporation as a whole has benefited from obtaining program-related capital investments at below-market rates from foundations but otherwise has very commercial methods of operation.

The Skills Needed to Sail Commercial Waters

If nonprofits are to explore commercial options, it is essential both that they build business capabilities and that they manage organizational culture. Management skills are important for all nonprofit organizations, but commercialization calls for expertise, knowledge, and attitudes more commonly found in the business world. Nonprofit managers need to become trained in business methods if they are to explore commercial options effectively. One way to gain such training is to reach out for help. Nonprofit managers can begin in their own backyards by finding more effective ways to draw on board members with relevant business experience. The resulting exchange will be a learning experience for both parties. Business board members are often an underutilized source of management expertise, and they need coaching and coaxing to adapt their business frameworks to the context of a social enterprise. They must understand the risks of becoming too businesslike and of moving too quickly. Nonprofit leaders also can reach out for pro bono consulting from volunteer business-people or from business school students. And nonprofits exploring commercialization can form alliances with for-profit companies to provide complementary skills and training in business methods.

Without internal staff expertise, however, the advice of board members, consultants, and partners may not be worth much. The organization needs staff that can understand and implement the new agenda. Organizations can hire employees with business skills, but they will need to address the cultural conflicts and compensation problems that could arise. The new hires must be supported fully, and care must be taken to allow them to build credibility within the core culture. Nonprofit leaders should anticipate cultural conflict and find ways to turn such conflict into a healthy, creative tension. They need to identify where operating styles are likely to clash, and they may have to launch internal education and communications initiatives in order to minimize the harmful effects of conflict and to help staff members agree on appropriate operating styles.

Of course, nonprofit leaders could opt to segregate commercial activities from philanthropic operations. Such an approach should reduce conflict, provided that the separate units do not need to interact on a day-to-day basis. Even so, staff on the more philanthropic side of operations may view their commercial colleagues with animosity or envy. Compensation is one possible source of friction between the two cultures. New hires from the business world may require higher compensation than internal staff members with comparable levels of education and years of experience. Pay equity has to be dealt with explicitly, or it will fester.

A former Wall Street banker who now heads a major international economic-development organization is grappling with precisely this issue. His operations have become increasingly sophisticated and require skills typically held by MBA graduates who could land investment-banking jobs. But he cannot pay anything approaching the investment-banking salaries to acquire the talent he needs. It was a challenge to get his board to let him make offers at salaries less than half those that qualified candidates could command in mainstream financial institutions. Yet even those salaries were well above existing wages in the organization, and the leader was concerned about pay equity with the organization's current staff. Raising everyone's salary could be extremely costly. Not doing so could undermine morale.

Engineering a new culture is never easy or quick. Building internal expertise has to be a deliberate strategic process. It cannot be accomplished overnight. Managers must create a new culture that blends commercial values with the traditional philanthropic principles that drive the organization. At the same time, they must work with key stakeholders to build understanding of and support for commercial activities, or they may find themselves in the awkward position that the AMA faced in its deal with Sunbeam.

Nonprofit leaders also need to get legal and tax advice before launching any commercial activities. Unfortunately, tax laws often lag behind industry developments. It is not always clear how current Internal Revenue Service regulations will treat new hybrid forms of organizations. In some cases, it will be better to set up a for-profit subsidiary and pay the appropriate taxes. As the boundaries between nonprofit and for-profit organizations fade, pressure will mount for new regulations and possible revisions in the tax code. Becoming more commercial has political risks and puts the burden of proof on social entrepreneurs to show that their organizations are serving social missions that justify continued tax exemption.

––––––––––

Thoughtful innovation in the social sector is essential if organizations are to leverage limited philanthropic resources. Nonprofit leaders can benefit from finding effective ways to harness commercial forces for social good. But misguided efforts to reinvent nonprofits in the image of business can go wrong. Nonprofit managers are only beginning to learn what it means to search for new solutions to social problems and for more effective ways to deliver socially important goods.

Strategic and structural innovation should focus on improving mission-related performance. Caught up in the current wave of commercialization, nonprofits risk forgetting that the most important measure of success is the achievement of mission-related objectives, not the financial wealth or stability of the organization. The benefit of finding attractive sources of earned income lies more in the leverage this income provides than its sustainability. But generating more funds for ineffective or inefficient programs is not a productive use of resources. True social-sector entrepreneurs are those who find not only additional sources of funds but also new methods to link funding to performance. More important, they develop more effective ways to improve conditions on this planet. To that end, social entrepreneurs shouldn't focus on commercial approaches alone but should explore all strategic options along the social enterprise spectrum, including their ability to use social causes to tap into philanthropic motivations. In fact, multi-unit operations may well be the wave of the future because they recognize and, when it makes sense, utilize a full range of options on the social enterprise spectrum.

In the end, commercial operations will not—and should not—drive out philanthropic initiatives. Many worthwhile objectives cannot effectively be pursued by relying on market mechanisms alone. In any case, people tend to get something out of giving that they cannot get out of market transactions. People want to make contributions to the common good, or to their vision of it. The challenge is to harness these social impulses and marry them to the best aspects of business practice in order to create a social sector that is as effective as it can be.

Originally published in January–February 1998. Reprint 98105

Note

The author would like to thank Elaine Backman for her contributions to the development of the social enterprise spectrum.

An Interview with Wynton Marsalis

Wynton Marsalis *grew up in a family of New Orleans jazz musicians and received his first trumpet as a sixth birthday present from bandleader Al Hirt. At 14 he debuted with the Louisiana Philharmonic; at 17 he moved to New York, where he attended Juilliard, joined Art Blakey's Jazz Messengers, assembled his own band, and began a prolific composing and recording career. In 1987, Marsalis founded Jazz at Lincoln Center.* **Interviewed by Katherine Bell**

HBR: *Why did you pick the trumpet?*

Marsalis: I got a trumpet for my sixth birthday, but I didn't practice it. And then the summer I was 12, I started listening to John Coltrane, and I wanted to play. There was so much racism when we grew up, and that's part of what inspired me; I wanted to represent my humanity. The work ethic I developed at that time— I still have that.

How did you learn to lead?

I was always a leader on teams. I called the plays in football, pitched baseball, played point guard in basketball. The guys would always ask me, "Man, what do you think we ought to do?"

When I was young I was too harsh on the musicians. The people who played with me taught me how to be better. I learned to have a clear direction. If you are wishy-washy or you lack heart, they can't follow you. It's exactly like leading on a horn. I play fourth trumpet, following Ryan Kisor. He's young, but a great lead player. He lets you know what he's going to play before he plays it. If everything's falling apart, he comes in. You can depend on him.

How is leading a band like running a company?

You have to know what your people can do. The ones who need to be challenged, you give them challenges. The ones who need to be carried, you carry them. The ones you need to let go, you let them go. A leader has got to have a certain kindness but a certain meanness, too.

What's your theory on talent versus practice?

You can become proficient at anything. If you're a boxer, you can practice four million hours and become proficient to a certain point, but if you don't have the talent, you won't be the one to beat. You can't practice the ability to make connections or have a deep, spiritual insight. To be great, you need courage to speak out and endurance to deal with what is given to you. Ornette Coleman got beat up for playing his music, but he played it. That's not something you can practice your way into.

How do you hire musicians?

I look for four things: First, individuality. Do they have a unique sound? Second, knowledge of the music. Third, do they respond well to pressure? And fourth, do they want to be a part of us?

Do you think about how somebody will fit into the group?

People with difficult personalities can survive in our world. If they can play, we embrace them and we work with them. But that doesn't mean they become less difficult.

Do you need to be alone to compose?

I grew up in a big family with a lot of noise. I like distraction. As a matter of fact, if I'm composing, I'll turn the television on. It makes me concentrate more deeply on what I'm doing.

Why did you decide to take on such a big management role with Lincoln Center?

My overall goal is to raise the level of artistic consciousness in our country, so that we become a country of the arts. To the day I die I want to work on that. I could go out and play and make much more money and have a much better time, but the work we do is important work. And I've learned so much doing it.

What's been the biggest challenge in building a major cultural institution from scratch?

Getting the level of financial support that the music deserves. That would be number one. We're constantly trying to find money to do arts programs. And when you have financial strain, you start to make decisions that are not the most prudent best-quality decisions. I'm not saying that we have done that, but it's a pressure.

You've been criticized a lot for taking a conservative approach to jazz.

I like being critiqued. I always knew I was original. If anything, the criticism made me more determined to go in my own direction. You have to assess criticism and then make your own decisions. You have to say, "We're going this way." That's what steels your leadership— you survive and become a better leader. If you can't take it, you're not the leader.

How much do you think about what the audience wants to hear?

I always think about what the audience wants to hear—and what they need to hear. What do I have to give people to bring them into the feeling of this music? The audience has got to really want to be there. Shakespeare had the right equation. He gave you sexuality and skullduggery and backstabbing, and then he gave you artistry, too. The high and low.

What can leaders learn from listening to jazz?

If you hone your listening skills so that you can follow the development of a solo, you can listen more empathetically to people when they talk and hear underneath what they're saying. You can feel their intention.

What has composing taught you about creativity?

Celebrate your traditions as you innovate. As you come up with new things, always reach back. Offer everything you have all the time.

Originally published in January–February 2011. Reprint R1101S

State Street's CEO on Creating Employment for At-Risk Youths

by Joseph Hooley

IN 2014 THE MASSACHUSETTS GOVERNOR'S OFFICE called and asked me to serve in a public/private partnership. The group hoped to improve the quality of community colleges in the Commonwealth. Workforce development is an issue I care about, and every CEO gets calls like this from time to time. I try to help out when I can, so I said yes.

I went to a few meetings, and I quickly became frustrated. This wasn't my first experience with public/private partnerships, and although some have been very successful, too many have not worked well. It can be mind-numbing. As I sat in one meeting, I began day-dreaming about how State Street might have the leverage to attack parts of the workforce development problem itself.

Our company has a large charitable foundation, so we were already spending millions of dollars a year in the areas of education and job training. State Street is one of Boston's largest employers, and we hire thousands of entry-level employees each year. That's important. The grand prize at the end of one's education is a job and a career, and we can provide that in a way that nonprofits can't.

Furthermore, our company is loaded with Millennials who want to volunteer, and mentorship is a key part of helping young people run the gamut from an urban high school to college and then into a job. When it comes to finding someone at State Street to mentor a student, you don't have to ask twice.

I began talking about this idea inside the company, and employees were enthusiastic. We wanted to go beyond spot solutions and put together a comprehensive, systematic, and scalable program—one aimed at producing measurable, sustained outcomes.

That's how we came to develop Boston WINs, which stands for "workforce investment network." We launched it in 2015, and we committed to investing $20 million and hiring 1,000 graduates of urban schools over the next four years. So far, the results are promising—we've hired more than 200 graduates, and they are proving to be an excellent fit with our culture. Outside the company, every business leader I've talked to has been intrigued by our model.

Urban Education Is Central

I think a lot about economic opportunity, because I come from a middle-class family. I grew up outside Boston, one of five siblings. When I was in college, I always had a part-time job, and I funded my education with loans and my own earnings. I was paying back student loans well into my thirties.

My dad worked at State Street for 32 years, but during most of his career here, the company was very different from what it is today. In the 1970s State Street was beginning to transform from a traditional bank into a technology-driven financial services company.

That shift made it attractive to me. After college I'd gone to work for AT&T, where I received extensive training in what we now call information technology. I met my wife during one of those classes. After the consent decree that broke up the old Bell system, I ended up working for American Bell, which was selling communications equipment to big organizations and competing against companies such as IBM. The technology bent stayed with me; I became focused

Idea in Brief

Frustrated by some of his experience with public/private partnerships, the author began daydreaming about how State Street, which has a large charitable foundation, could attack the problem of workforce development. The foundation was already spending millions of dollars a year in the areas of education and job training, and State Street is one of Boston's largest employers: It could provide a job and a career at the end of a young person's education, which nonprofits could not. Furthermore, the company is full of Millennials who want to volunteer as mentors.

In 2015 Hooley and his team launched Boston WINs ("workforce investment networks"). They committed to investing $20 million and hiring 1,000 graduates of urban schools over the next four years.

on finding ways to use technology to enable services and create capabilities.

My father retired from State Street in December 1985, and I joined one month later. I spent 10 years running a State Street joint venture, initially in Kansas City. I returned to Boston in 2000 to lead our global investment services business and was eventually promoted to vice chairman and then president. In 2010 I became State Street's CEO.

Along the way, I became involved in local philanthropy, particularly as an active supporter and a board member of the Boys & Girls Clubs of Boston. I was able to visit some of the clubs to see their good work. They provide after-school care, teach skills, organize sports teams, and help kids with homework. I saw how much good organizations like that can do. I also worked on some urban school initiatives in which State Street had become involved.

Through that work I became convinced that if I could help fix just one problem in the world, it would be urban education. Societal problems tend to be interconnected, and urban education touches many of them. Improving it creates economic growth, reduces crime, and lessens unemployment, social strife, and homelessness. I've visited a lot of schools over the years, and I've seen some excellent ones, but the solutions to providing good urban education tend to be spotty, and they don't scale well.

Working Like a Relay Race

The more I thought about the problem, the more I recognized that to be effective, our approach needed to go beyond what happens in urban classrooms. Getting students through school, into college, and then into good jobs requires managing a series of handoffs and transitions, just as runners in a relay race have to pass the baton. For example, some nonprofits do a great job of coaching high school students to improve their study skills or to perform better on college admissions exams. But rarely do those same organizations help the students with the college search and application process, which is the logical next step. Other organizations do that, but many kids can't navigate between the two. Then, when students get into college, they need mentoring and coaching to help them stay enrolled and succeed, which requires a different kind of support. After that they need help getting ready for a job and finding one. It's similar to a hospital experience: The patient may be treated by several specialists, and they have to communicate well with one another to achieve overall success.

We wanted to create a program that would combine all the kinds of expertise necessary to support youths through high school and college and into the workforce. The key would be a coordinated system to pass students between these specialties, rather than relying on the students themselves to find what they needed when they needed it in a patchwork of organizations and solutions.

In short, we wanted to bring together a handful of nonprofits with a proven record of getting and keeping students on the path from the education system to employment, give those nonprofits funding to scale up, coordinate their efforts so that they were no longer working in isolation, and then commit to hiring a large number of those students after graduation.

The Five Partners

With that vision in place, the question became: How would we achieve it?

Through State Street's charitable foundation, we already had relationships with organizations that excelled at addressing specific pieces of the larger problem. But we decided to open up the field. We created a request for proposals and then held a *Shark Tank*–like competition among nonprofits, with the goal of choosing five groups that would receive grants over four years. Nonprofits crave multi-year funding commitments, so we had no problem getting a number of them to compete.

Not until they got involved in our screening process did they realize how hard this would be. To become a part of Boston WINs, they'd need to start collaborating with other organizations, which isn't necessarily their strength. Many of the highest-performing, most dynamic nonprofits have charismatic leaders; we were asking them to check their egos at the door and focus on ways to collaborate. That didn't always come naturally. My primary feedback to everyone was that the groups needed to think bigger. I believe that's part of a leader's role—to force people to raise their level of ambition.

We ended up choosing four organizations we'd funded previously and one that was new to us. Year Up is a Boston-based national organization that provides intensive skills training for low-income young adults. UAspire focuses on helping students find ways to finance college. The Boston Private Industry Council (PIC) helps students obtain workplace experience and find a path from school to work. College Advising Corps (CAC) assists students with the college search and application process. And Bottom Line helps low-income and first-generation students get to and through college.

Although the five organizations remain separate, we expect them to work closely—not unlike a group of manufacturing suppliers that need to cooperate so that parts fit together perfectly, deliveries are synchronized, and quality remains high. We call this *coordinated action,* and it refers to our intention to deliver these services in a complementary, reinforcing, and properly sequenced manner. We closely track what services each student is receiving; all five partners enter their data into a shared system every two weeks. We have 20 high schools participating this year; at each one we hold a monthly meeting where reps from the five organizations discuss individual students' progress. All the students have a list of 12 milestones they must reach by certain dates—such as submitting college essays, completing financial aid forms, participating in a job shadow program, drafting a résumé, and doing a mock interview. Coordinated action allows us to confirm that students are staying on track, identify those who may have a gap in the support they're receiving, and ensure that effective handoffs are taking place between the various organizations, especially when students make the big leap from high school into college.

The Broad Reach of Boston WINs

After the five nonprofits were chosen, we brought them in for a day-long session that I attended. We made sure everybody was committed to the vision. They were all enthusiastic—after all, they'd just won in a competitive setting. The challenge was that these organizations are used to having control. We had to explain that this would be different—each organization would need to hand clients off to another organization, and the goal was to maximize the collective impact of all five.

I cannot overemphasize how hard that has proved to be. Each of these nonprofits had been operating in its own lane and had perfected a solution to a piece of the problem. We were trying to get them to think and work holistically and horizontally in ways they hadn't before.

We launched the program in June 2015, at an event with Boston Mayor Marty Walsh and Massachusetts Governor Charlie Baker. It was a wonderful culmination of the first stage of the program. But it was just the beginning.

The beauty of Boston WINs is that it can reach any city youth who is involved with one of the five organizations, all of which had recruitment processes in place before they partnered with State Street. (Year Up and Bottom Line have a formal application system, whereas services provided by uAspire, PIC, and CAC are available to any eligible Boston public school student.) Because the existing system of each nonprofit was already working well, we decided not

"It Was Vital to Have That Support"

When Alana Hans-Bodden was attending public school in the Boston neighborhood of Dorchester, she believed she was smart enough to become the first in her family to go to college. But the steps involved—from choosing the right school to applying to lining up financial aid—were overwhelming. Hans-Bodden, now a 24-year-old senior associate on State Street's independent verification team, obtained help from a nonprofit called Bottom Line, which is part of the Boston WINs program. She explains how it helped her get ahead. Edited excerpts follow:

When did you begin working with Bottom Line? I started in high school. They worked with me on college applications, essays, interviews, and financial aid and scholarship applications. They try to make sure you find the best fit for college. I attended Bridgewater State University, and a Bottom Line counselor worked with me throughout my time there. We had formal meetings three times every semester—at the beginning, at midterms, and right before finals. Bottom Line also held career fairs and helped me write a résumé and prepare for job interviews.

Would you have made it to college without that assistance? I think so. But I probably would have taken a break from college when my mom passed. I was a 20-year-old sophomore, and I became responsible for my 12-year-old sister. Bottom Line helped streamline things for me—how to fill out the right forms, send the right e-mails to my professors, and notify people so that I could get through that semester and stay enrolled. It was vital to have that support.

How did you wind up at State Street? My first interaction with State Street was at a career fair, as a freshman in college. At the time, I was a political science major who wanted to go to law school, and finance wasn't on my radar. But my mother was an accountant, and not long before she died, we had a conversation about how a finance or accounting major would benefit me in the long run, particularly since law school would be difficult to afford. I talked to my Bottom Line counselor, and she suggested I do a job shadow. I spent a day watching someone work at State Street. Late in my senior year, I was asked to give a speech at a dinner for Bottom Line. After I spoke, a State Street HR person approached me and began introducing me to executives. I interned there during the summer of 2015 and joined full-time that fall. My work is challenging—it's not the same thing every day. I have to think about work processes and analyze data to find ways the company can reduce risk and increase compliance.

What's your involvement with Boston WINs now? I keep in touch with my Bottom Line counselors, I go to events, and I network within State Street with other employees who've come through the programs that make up Boston WINs. Looking back, I see that I came away from my experience with more confidence, a better sense of what I wanted to do with my life, and a better ability to connect, to be myself, and to reach out for support when I need it.

to interfere; instead, any student working with any of the five is automatically considered a Boston WINs youth. The new program connects the five nonprofits so that a student who receives assistance from College Advising Corps in searching for and applying to colleges will now also receive guidance on financing his or her education from uAspire. In its first year alone, Boston WINs served more than 19,430 youths, and State Street hired 216 Boston WINs graduates.

We opened a facility at the University of Massachusetts that allows students to work part-time, gaining job experience and giving us a look at how they work. We have more than 50 interns from Bunker Hill Community College at any given time. We give them a tryout, and we hire some of them permanently after they graduate. Once they're on board, they can develop their skills and migrate through the organization.

We've committed to four years of funding, but we evaluate each nonprofit annually to see how well it's contributing to the overall mission. We reserve the right to kick a group out if it's not cooperating. We measure progress using metrics and dashboards. We want to see how many people are affected by these programs and how their trajectories have improved. When you're looking at scale and return on investment, the metrics are important, but the individual results are important too. When you meet a kid whose trajectory was completely changed by a program like this, it's inspiring. And those young people work hard as employees. They appreciate that the opportunity they've been given is something special.

Not Just Feel-Good Stuff

As a CEO, I'm careful about how much time I devote to philanthropy. I report to our 11-person board of directors, and I'm responsible to shareholders, employees, clients, and the community. My greatest allocation of time is to the first three groups, as you'd expect. But the link between our community involvement and my own conscience is pretty tight. This is not just feel-good stuff. We're competing for talent in this city, and all our employees—especially the younger ones—appreciate our community involvement. I meet every month for breakfast with groups of employees, and I always ask them two questions: What keeps you at State Street? and What would prevent you from staying at State Street? They usually cite flexible working conditions, career opportunities, and community involvement as their priorities. The connection between that community involvement and our employees translates directly into how well we serve our shareholders and clients.

We're nearly halfway through our four-year commitment to Boston WINs, and I think we've established a pretty good rhythm. We're already thinking about how to scale the program beyond Boston, to other parts of the country and the world. State Street has big operations in Kansas City, Singapore, Poland, Ireland, and elsewhere, and there's no reason we can't make it work in those places, too.

The program fits nicely with the evolution of our company's strategy. As CEO, my two biggest priorities have been to transform State Street into a technology-enabled digital business and to make us less about processing and more about deriving success from data and analytics. That strategy shift has had an impact on our hiring. We need employees who are very comfortable with data and know how to analyze it. We need more IT workers. As a result of the Great Recession and the Troubled Asset Relief Program, companies like ours also face more regulation, so we're hiring staffers in the compliance function as well. Boston WINs is helping us find great employees in these areas.

I believe that Boston WINs will be an important part of what State Street accomplishes during this decade. If we can crack the code on the problem of urban workforce development, we'll create a diverse group of well-educated and highly motivated employees for our company while also filling a need for the entire community. Companies talk a lot about wanting new hires to be "job ready," and Boston WINs achieves that. It's a great example of how a program that benefits the city can simultaneously benefit our shareholders.

Originally published in May–June 2017. Reprint R1703A

An Interview with Salman Khan

Salman Khan *was working as a hedge fund analyst when he started using online tools to tutor his cousins in math. Nine years later, his nonprofit organization, Khan Academy, draws on the same approach to offer more than 5,000 free, web-based video lessons to millions of students across the globe, disrupting not only schools but also the education industry built around them.* **Interviewed by Alison Beard**

HBR: *What are the key concepts students should understand in order to be successful in today's workplace?*

Khan: The one meta-level thing is to take agency over your own learning. In the traditional academic model, you're passive. You sit in a chair, and the teacher tries to project knowledge at you; some of it sticks, some of it doesn't. That's not an effective way to learn. Worse, it creates a mind-set of "you need to teach me," so when you're on your own, you think, "I can't learn." Anyone in any industry will tell you there's new stuff to learn every week these days. So you have to say, "What information and people do I have at my disposal? What questions do I need to ask? How do I gauge whether I've really understood it?" Khan Academy is designed to give students that agency. If you want to get more tangible, I would say learn how to program a computer, more about the law, and definitely statistics.

In your book, you talk about curiosity being stamped out of kids. How do you bring it back?

Curiosity is a hard thing to squash, but the traditional model of education manages pretty well: Listen to lectures, take notes, feed back what you learned, and then forget it all. You're not allowed to go beyond the curriculum. Khan Academy is all about giving more breathing room. You want to go deep? Go deep. I had this to some degree at the public school I went to in Louisiana, where there were gifted programs. Every day, starting in second grade, they took me out of class for an hour, and I would go to another room, with a mixed age group. The first time I went, I thought it was the biggest racket. I walked up to Miss Rouselle's desk, and she asked, "What do you like to do?" I was like, I'm seven years old—shouldn't you be telling me what to do? But I said, "I like to draw. I like puzzles." She said, "OK, have you used oil paints? Have you done Mind Benders?" Soon I looked forward to that hour more than I did to spending the night at my friend's house. And I learned more that applies to what I do today than in the five other hours of the day combined.

That's what we need to create space for. Historically, it was hard to do in a scalable way. How do you personalize education for 30 kids without breaking the bank? But technology can deliver information at a student's pace, give practice problems and feedback, and arm teachers with data, so that when students go into a classroom, it's much more like what I experienced in that gifted program.

How much of what you've learned about effective education applies to the business world?

The idea that you do K–12, four years of college, maybe some grad school, and then stop learning is a myth. The book applies to life-long learning: Go at your own pace, master content before moving on, and do it without disrupting your current work and productivity. A lot of corporations, when they do training, mimic the classroom. They create corporate universities; people have to take time off and listen to lectures. But the information and credentials you get coming out of those classes aren't as useful as other things. At Khan Academy, when we hire, it's nice if you have a high GPA and an academically rigorous major. But what we really care about is what you've made. For engineers, show us software you've designed. We also want evidence of how you work with other people, the leadership you exhibit, and what your peers think of you.

Your findings on the limits of human concentration seem relevant too.

We think that because this generation has Facebook, Twitter, and mobile phones, they don't have attention spans. But it's clear from the studies that we never really had the attention spans the classroom-based lecture model expects of students. Especially with dense subject matter, humans can pay attention for 10 to 15 minutes before they zone out. You zone back in for eight or nine minutes, then you zone out again. The zoning in gets shorter; the zoning out gets longer. By the end of the hour you might have picked up 30% of the material—or you might be lost altogether. That has consequences in a work setting, too. If people are meeting, they don't need a lecture; if you don't need them to interact, information should just be in a video or a memo. At Khan Academy, one side effect of that approach is we've created a library of videos that provide background on our thinking, so that we can tell a new employee, "Go watch." We make videos for our board, too, so that everyone can see that historical narrative; then the board meetings are mainly interactive Q&A.

Should every company use videos instead of memos?

There's something you get only from a human voice—little intuitions or parentheticals that people express verbally but for some reason not in a white paper or a memo. It's incredibly valuable.

You've been called the world's teacher. How much of that came to you intuitively, and how much did you learn along the way?

If you're being talked down to in a classroom, or if a lecture is over your head, you feel belittled. As my wife will tell you, I'm hypersensitive to that. When someone uses an even slightly exasperated tone, my reaction is, "Hey, don't talk to me that way!" So when I give a talk, 10% or 15% of my brain is thinking, "Sal, are you sounding arrogant? Are you talking down to people, or above them?"

Also, I've always been interested in really understanding things. When you have a strong foundation, everything falls into place a lot easier later on. I don't say, "Memorize this formula." I say, "This is how my brain thinks about it." I try to make my thought process very transparent; if I'm doing calculus or quantitative finance, I'm not afraid to remind myself of some basic arithmetic.

Your first trial-and-error attempts to teach your cousins remind me of the iterative "lean start-up" model.

You have to do some planning, but you get real information only when you put something out there, observe people using it, get data, and quickly iterate to throw something else out. One thing in my mind is to not lose that.

Now that you have more people, and solid funding, why have you stuck with the same model—your voice against a simple digital blackboard?

When I started making videos, in 2006, I did 10 or 20 as a proof of concept, and, with my MBA hat on, I thought, "I'll get a bunch of other people to make content, because that's the only way to address all the topics I want to." But it was hard to find people to participate, and I realized I could scale up on my own far more than I had assumed. Within two or three months I had done 80 or 90 algebra videos. Then I moved on to geometry and calculus and physics. But I'm clearly not going to be able to cover everything, and people might appreciate a different style. We have a few other folks already doing art history, medicine, and project-based learning videos, and we've hired a team to build the tools and platform to allow more people to create content. You're going to see content in many languages. You're going to see us going much deeper into interactive experiences.

When your lessons are criticized, how do you respond?

You have to figure out what is meaningful and constructive and what isn't. When someone sends us an e-mail or writes a blog post about something they think is incorrect or unhelpful, and they're right, we annotate or redo the video. That's one of the values of this form over a traditional textbook, where you get little or no feedback. When we put content out, 10,000 people look at it within a week.

It's a very fast editorial cycle. We don't have to wait until the next textbook. We can fix it overnight.

Khan Academy is clearly disrupting education. Will you kill off some established players?

Whether or not Khan Academy exists, the world in which a business model is based on charging people for access to information—and not even new information, but 300-year-old science or math—is going away. I think publishers recognize that and see that there are opportunities for them. They already have huge distribution and traction in schools globally. If they turned those schools into registered internet users and customized material for them, the market would value that. It's not 100% clear how to monetize it, especially since we're out here saying that access to learning is a human right. But the writing's on the wall.

At the same time, there are start-ups trying to imitate your model on a for-profit basis.

The more dollars thrown at the problem, the better. If a for-profit player gives away part of an education in order to attract customers, that's a win for everyone.

Why did you set Khan Academy up as a nonprofit?

In the for-profit realm, a home run is to scale big, get 100 million users, and go public or get acquired. That would have been good for me individually and for our investors. But it felt a little wrong, because I wanted our content to be accessible to all people, for a long time into the future. Beyond your generation, do you have confidence that a for-profit will stay true to its mission? The institutions that have had global reach over multiple generations have been not-for-profits. That's a home run in that sector. And maybe Khan Academy can be one of those. In terms of its advantages, we get goodwill. There are 51 people in the organization, plus thousands of volunteers, and we're attracting some of the best in Silicon Valley: McKinsey folks, people from Google and Facebook, one of the leading quant fund guys, the world's top Java script programmer. These incredible people come for the mission, not even realizing that we actually pay pretty well. So we're getting a caliber I don't think anyone else can.

What kind of boss are you?

It's an exciting and hard challenge: How do you have a flat and nimble structure? How can you be approachable but also have authority? How do you make sure people's voices are heard while correcting something you feel is going in the wrong direction? Every manager has to plot his own trajectory and be as open to feedback as possible.

Eventually you're going to run into another classic management problem: You're the face of the organization. Can the Academy exist without you?

Two years ago that would have been impossible. Even now a lot of the press narrative is about me tutoring my cousins and making videos. But that's starting to change, because people see our inter-active platform, which was clearly worked on by people other than me. As we bring other content creators on board, my hope is that I can continue to be a valuable evangelist for what we're doing. But if, God forbid, I get hit by a bus, Khan Academy should sur-vive. We have a deep bench. I'm the least impressive person in the organization.

A lot of us dream of leaving our jobs to do something good for the world. How did you decide to take the plunge?

I really enjoyed my hedge fund job; it was far more thought pro-voking and intellectual than people might assume. But I also found a lot of satisfaction working with my cousins, writing the software, and making the videos. So in the back of my mind, I thought I would become a portfolio manager, have my own fund, and maybe 15 or 20 years in the future, on my own terms, fund a school. As anyone in investments will tell you, you have bad days, and you think maybe you should do your hobby full-time. But then you remember you don't own a house, you have a baby on the way, and you haven't paid off your or your wife's student loans, so you stop dreaming. I'd been part of the dot-com bubble, and I found it so exhausting emotionally that I told myself entrepreneurship was not for me. So when I started Khan Academy, I said, "This is a hobby. This is a passion. This is fun." And I protected it that way as it developed. I thank my old boss, because he thought it was valuable for us to have our own lives, and that created a space for Khan Academy to blossom. When I took the plunge, it was significantly de-risked. By 2009, 100,000 people were using the videos, we'd been on CNN and in *USA Today,* and I was starting to talk to philanthropists. So I sat down with my wife and said, "Let's give it a year. If I can't get it off the ground, I can go back to my old job." Nine months in, things started to happen.

You're backed by the likes of Bill Gates and Carlos Slim. What have you learned from them?

All of them, even though they sit on top of empires, go deep and try to understand things themselves. They're very hands-on. And they're incredibly curious. The first time I met Carlos Slim, we sat on a beach for four hours and talked about what civilizations existed during previous interglacial periods. These people are big thinkers. Seeing that has given me the confidence to let my epic juices flow, so to speak—to indulge my science fiction, delusional dreams. You have to, for some of your stuff to become a reality.

Your wife is a doctor, and you have two young children. How do you balance work and family?

I set hard lines. Weekends are for my family. I do not touch the computer unless it is an absolute emergency. When I come back on Monday, I'm refreshed and productive. The same goes for evenings. I've been up on stage at speaking events and said, "I have to go give my kids a bath now," and everyone is shocked. But if I can't have dinner with my kids, give them a bath, and read them a book before bed, something is wrong in my life.

Originally published in January–February 2014. Reprint R1401M

Do Better at Doing Good

by V. Kasturi Rangan, Sohel Karim, and
Sheryl K. Sandberg

Editor's Note: *Articles throughout this volume explore the variations between effective practices at nonprofit and for-profit organizations. These can play out most drastically in the marketing department: when a social-change initiative provides a significant personal benefit to a buyer, conventional marketing methods—such as those used for marketing consumer goods—can be successful. But when costs are high and personal benefits are intangible (lowering personal carbon emissions, to use a current example), social marketers face their greatest challenges.*

In this piece the authors present a foundational framework for designing a social-change campaign. The framework is intended to help nonprofit leaders decide when standard marketing methods are appropriate and when an alternative approach is needed. Despite being written before social media radically changed nonprofit marketing tactics (ironic, as Sheryl Sandberg, who later became world-famous as COO of Facebook, coauthored this piece soon after completing her MBA), the takeaways from "Do Better at Doing Good" about understanding human motivations are fundamental, timeless, and applicable to any marketing campaign.

IN THE MID-1980S, SEVERAL major antidrug initiatives, targeted at school-age children, were launched in Boston. A significant amount of media time and space was devoted to public-service announcements designed by top-notch advertising talents. The ads were brief, clear, and informative. In 1987, however, market surveys revealed that although many people remembered the campaigns, the effort at social change had been, in large part, unsuccessful. The initiatives did not persuade their target audience to change its behavior. What went wrong? Should the managers spearheading the various campaigns have known better? Could they have planned more effective strategies from the outset?

Quite often, managers in charge of developing marketing strategies for social-change efforts—such as antidrug campaigns, community development programs, or recycling initiatives—rely on conventional, consumer-goods-oriented marketing methods to promote their missions. Unfortunately, such methods are not always effective. Conventional marketing methods are generally designed for situations in which benefits to the consumer from choosing the advertised product or service clearly outweigh the costs. Choosing a particular credit-card company because it offers a low interest rate is a clear-cut proposition with a tangible reward. So is purchasing an automobile with a certain set of features. With social marketing, however, the benefits are not always so concrete. They often accrue to society, sometimes over the long term. In fact, in some cases, the individuals, communities, or organizations targeted by the change effort may feel that the costs of change exceed the benefits.

For example, most people in the developed world are well aware of the harmful consequences of deforestation. Yet one would hardly expect a logging laborer in Brazil to stop cutting trees, even if the long-term consequences of his actions were made clear to him. If he changed his behavior, he would no longer be able to support his family.

Clearly, not all social-marketing programs are bedeviled by a what's-in-it-for-me reaction from their intended targets. But many are, and such attitudes must be dealt with. We have developed a framework to help social marketers determine which causes can be promoted through conventional marketing methods, which need an alternative approach, and what the options are in the latter case.

Idea in Brief

In spite of top-notch efforts, many social-change initiatives fail. What goes wrong? How can the initiatives be presented more effectively? Analyzing the costs and benefits of the proposed change from the perspective of the targeted community can help marketers answer those questions. The authors present a framework to facilitate such an analysis and to help form effective marketing plans.

When the proposed behavior change involves little cost to the targeted community and provides a significant personal benefit, conventional market methods—such as those used for marketing consumer goods—can be effective. The task becomes more challenging when the targeted community cannot perceive an immediate personal benefit and thus lacks the motivation to change its behavior. In such cases, it may be possible to overcome the inertia by making the proposed change as easy as possible to implement.

When the proposed change involves a high cost, in terms of either money or some other measure (difficulty, for instance, in quitting smoking), the social marketer's job becomes harder. The campaign must not only communicate effectively, it must also provide any support that the targeted community will need in order to comply.

Social marketers face their greatest challenge in cases where the cost is high and the personal benefit is intangible. In some instances, it may be possible for the marketers to change the focus of the campaign; another approach is to persuade a small portion of the targeted community to change their behavior and then leverage the power of those early adopters. Moral persuasion and peer pressure can help over the long term as well.

Obstacles to Marketing Social Change

Before introducing our framework for assessing social-marketing challenges and planning effective campaigns, we must consider the obstacles facing social marketers in greater detail.

To begin with, in many social-marketing situations, *the target community opposes the change being advocated*. Social change often involves altering people's core attitudes and beliefs as a prelude to changing their behavior. Consider the issue of family planning in Bangladesh. In the late 1970s, government officials determined that the small country, which is the size of the state of Wisconsin, would soon outgrow its limited economic resources if it did not control its population growth rate. With the help of foreign aid, the government launched a massive campaign to curb population growth. Contraceptives for men were given out free at clinics and social workers urged men to practice family planning.

The effort fell short. Why? Because most of the country's citizens did not understand the long-term benefits to the country; they saw only the conflicts between the proposed behavior changes and their way of life, and the problems that such change would bring upon them as individuals. Most parents counted on children to be a support in their old age, because Bangladesh, like many developing nations, does not have a system of pensions or social security for all its citizens. Since many Bangladeshi children die before they reach adulthood—the result of natural calamities such as typhoons and epidemics such as cholera—couples usually had a few "extra" children as a safety margin. Also, in the Bangladeshi social system, tradition dictates that the parents of the bride present the parents of the groom with a cash gift at the wedding, so it made sense to try to have at least as many male children as female to balance the cash flow. Furthermore, a large family would provide sufficient hands for cultivating rice and catching fish, avoiding the necessity of hiring labor outside the family. Finally, there were those among the country's predominantly Muslim population who viewed family planning as an unnatural act that violated their religious faith. It is no wonder the initial campaign was unsuccessful.

Another common obstacle to social change is that, for the target community, *the adoption costs often exceed tangible benefits.* That is certainly the case for the logger—or the logging company—in Brazil being asked to give up work (or profits) to save the rain forest. The same holds true for chemical companies that are asked to stop producing chlorofluorocarbons (CFCs) to protect the earth's fragile ozone layer.

CFCs have been unequivocally identified as destructive of the ozone layer. If CFC production were stopped immediately, it is estimated that by the year 2075 some 3 million lives in the United States alone would be saved from death from skin cancer. Globally, the number would exceed 10 million lives saved. But for the chemical companies that produce CFCs, the cost of terminating production, researching and developing alternatives, and bringing those alternatives to market are an immediate, tangible concern. In 1989, those costs were estimated to be approximately $500 million for each of the dozen or so companies that would be affected. For chemical companies whose main business is producing CFCs, it is difficult to appreciate long-term, societal benefits in the face of the immediate cost, especially since it would be difficult for a third party—a government or foundation, for instance—to provide monetary compensation for ceasing CFC production.

With some social-marketing initiatives, a critical obstacle to implementation is that *early adopters stand to lose*. Again, consider the chemical companies. If only a few companies changed their behavior, those companies would be at a disadvantage in a marketplace where other organizations continued to make and market cheaper, yet environmentally dangerous, products.

Similarly, if only a few couples in Bangladesh chose to have smaller families, those couples would be at a disadvantage among their peers, and there would be no ensuing benefit to society. Schools would become less crowded, food more plentiful, and medical facilities widely available only if the society as a whole reduced its birthrate.

That obstacle brings to light another, related challenge. In conventional marketing situations, if some consumers balk at a new feature or service package, marketers have the option of segmenting the market—identifying and targeting those people for whom their product or service will be attractive. With social-marketing efforts, such flexibility is not always possible. In fact, with many social-change initiatives, *the benefit accrues only when a large percentage of the target community accepts the proposed change*. For example, even if a few chemical companies were more inclined than others to change their behavior, social marketers cannot limit their campaigns to persuading those few to change. The ozone layer's rate of depletion will not decrease measurably until all the major producers of CFCs are on board.

The type of initiative . . .

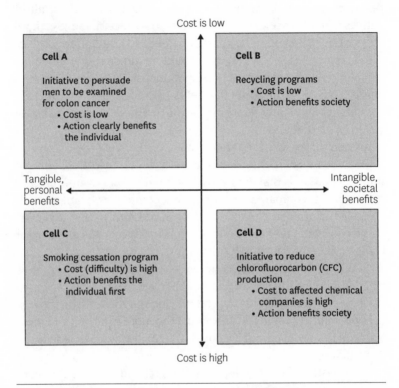

Cost is low

Cell A

Initiative to persuade
men to be examined
for colon cancer
 • Cost is low
 • Action clearly benefits
   the individual

Cell B

Recycling programs
 • Cost is low
 • Action benefits society

Tangible,
personal
benefits

Intangible,
societal
benefits

Cell C

Smoking cessation program
 • Cost (difficulty) is high
 • Action benefits the
   individual first

Cell D

Initiative to reduce
chlorofluorocarbon (CFC)
production
 • Cost to affected chemical
   companies is high
 • Action benefits society

Cost is high

Analyzing the Costs and Benefits of Change

We have developed a framework that allows social marketers to examine the change they are advocating from the potential adopter's perspective and to plan their marketing strategy accordingly. There are four cells located along a vertical axis that represents the cost dimension and a horizontal axis that represents the benefits. (See the chart "The type of initiative . . .")

By costs, we mean not only the monetary costs of adopting a behavior but also the costs in terms of time, effort, and any other psychological (or organizational) discomfort the adoption behavior

. . . and the challenge it presents

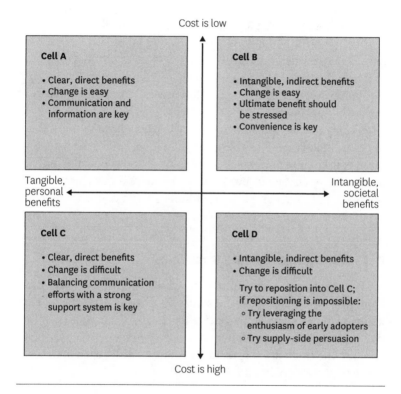

may cause. For example, the cost of smoking cessation is high because giving up cigarettes is tremendously difficult.

Similarly, the benefit dimension includes all nonmonetary advantages that individuals or organizations may gain if they adopt the recommended behavior. These advantages range from physiological benefits and psychological benefits at the individual level to improved corporate image for organizations and environmental or sociological benefits at a societal level.

A principal function of the benefit dimension is to identify the primary beneficiary of any given program for social change. A campaign designed to encourage men to be tested for colon cancer, for example, clearly benefits individuals; an AIDS prevention program, on the other hand, benefits not only the individuals toward whom the campaign is directed but also all potential partners of those individuals. With a recycling initiative, the primary beneficiary is the community or society as a whole. Of course, individuals gain if their community as a whole is better off, but the gain is felt primarily at a societal level and only secondarily at the individual level.

In many cases, the distinctions between beneficiaries are difficult to make; indeed, the lines between individual and societal benefits often overlap. Preventing or stopping drug abuse benefits individuals, but the change in behavior also fosters a healthier society. For marketing purposes, it is important to try to define the primary beneficiaries as specifically as possible.

Determining Appropriate Strategies

Once a manager has determined in which cell the initiative most appropriately belongs, the next step is to consider what kind of marketing plan will be most persuasive for that particular kind of initiative. Each cell presents different marketing problems. (See the chart ". . . and the challenge it presents.") Let us consider each of the cells in the framework individually.

Cell A

Here, the cost to the intended beneficiary of changing behavior is relatively small compared to the potential benefits. The task for marketers is thus similar to persuading consumers to buy conventional products and services. First, the marketer will need to concentrate on communicating the benefits of the proposed behavior change to the target community. Second, the marketer should make sure that any tools or services necessary for adopting the change are readily available.

Consider an initiative designed to persuade middle-aged men to visit their doctors for a colon cancer check. The campaign was created by the Advertising Council, a nonprofit agency based in New York that develops and places close to a billion dollars' worth of public-service announcements every year. Ad Council marketers knew that for a vast majority of males, adopting the behavior change would involve only the minor inconvenience of scheduling and keeping a doctor's appointment. After the examination, most of them would be declared cancer-free. For the unlucky few who would be diagnosed as having a potential cancer, the benefits of early medical attention and treatment would far outweigh the initial costs of making and keeping an appointment.

So the campaign took a conventional approach: It relied on communication to demonstrate the clear value of the change to the targeted individuals. The campaign's most important component was information dissemination. Success depended on the effectiveness of the communication and its reach. The target community—the "customers"—needed to know why it was important to get an early checkup. The campaign sought to create an urgency in the minds of the target population in order to stimulate them to arrange for examinations. Because most doctors and health professionals are well trained in the detection procedure, service availability was not a problem.

It is important to underscore that Cell A campaigns do not need to address deep-rooted beliefs or attitudes. The targets of Cell A campaigns often are merely complacent; they pass up the desired behavior not because they are opposed to it but because they do not have the information that would prompt them to change. But when information is presented, knowledge can quickly lead to persuasion.

Another note on Cell A endeavors: Many social-marketing campaigns unnecessarily oversell the morbid consequences of not adopting the recommended behavior. Some of them employ a heavy-handed tone in an attempt to change underlying attitudes, when simply providing information and support would be more effective. Instead of giving parents information on where and how to get their children immunized, for example, a campaign may get drawn into portraying the disastrous consequence of not adopting the behavior—a child's death. Infrequently, a "fear appeal" may be necessary to shock and goad people to action, but most money and time spent on such approaches are wasted resources—lost opportunities to persuade the audience more reasonably.

Cell B

As with Cell A projects, Cell B projects do not require fundamental shifts in the attitudes or lifestyles of the target population. The problem with Cell B projects is that they may not seem compelling; there are no direct, individual benefits. Marketers facing Cell B challenges need to focus their efforts on providing a catalyst for change in the form of a convenient way for the target population to comply.

Consider the problem of resource conservation at the household level. In the early 1990s, a survey conducted by the Environmental Federation of America (Earth Share) revealed that 74% of respondents supported stronger environmental standards, regardless of cost. This was a considerable jump from a similar survey conducted in the mid-1980s that had shown about 45% support for environmental initiatives. Yet market research company Roper Starch reported in 1992 that fewer than one in ten Americans made personal efforts on a regular basis to help solve environmental problems.

Earth Share, hoping to increase participation in resource conservation practices in homes nationwide, retained the Ad Council to develop a communications program supporting environmentally friendly behavior at the household level. The Ad Council's campaign team, in turn, commissioned its own survey of nearly 1,000 men and women to ascertain opinions of 20 environmentally friendly behaviors such as shutting off water while brushing teeth and using energy-efficient light-bulbs. The questions were designed to reveal how important, difficult, and demanding those behaviors seemed, how frequently respondents currently practiced them, and how willing they would be to start practicing the behaviors if they were not doing so currently.

The survey found that respondents were highly sensitive, in general, to environmental issues. Most of the behaviors covered by the survey were rated as highly important. Some of the behaviors (such as using cloth shopping bags or putting a bottle or brick in the toilet tank) were also perceived as easy to adopt. Surprisingly, however, respondents reported that they only rarely practiced these behaviors.

Based on the survey results, the Ad Council determined that the catalyst people needed to change their behavior was simply clear instruction about easy things they could do at home to protect the environment and frequent reminders to do them. So marketers launched a relentless communication campaign reminding the public to adopt the behaviors and showing them how to do so. Over the last few years, as the campaign has matured, the focus of the ads, brochures, and other methods of communication has become increasingly practical. The result has been a sharp increase in household-level conservation practices.

For the purposes of contrast, consider a Cell B challenge with very different parameters: one philanthropist's efforts to promote the development of rural areas in Thailand. With an average annual GNP growth rate of 10% or higher through the late 1980s and early 1990s, Thailand is one of the world's fastest-growing economies. Unfortunately, the disparity between personal incomes in the urban and rural sectors is growing at an even faster rate. The average annual per capita income in the Greater Bangkok area is about $3,000; in Thailand's other provinces, per capita income ranges from $300 to $1,000. In 1989, to address the imbalance, Mechai Viravaidya, a philanthropist known for his work on family planning issues, launched TBIRD: the Thai Business Initiative in Rural Development.

TBIRD had a simple plan. Large private companies doing business in Thailand would each be asked to "adopt" a village in the rural interior and assist in its development. Businesspeople would devote a given amount of time and resources to help villagers boost agricultural productivity and acquire skills in non-agricultural activities. As Mechai said shortly before TBIRD's launch, "If only business could be convinced to voluntarily devote a small portion of their time and resources to address a national development need, we would not need the assistance of bureaucrats and politicians."

But the idea did not take hold very easily. In the overall scheme of things, adopting a village would not be a financial drain on the resources of the large private companies that TBIRD was targeting, but direct benefits to those companies were hard to identify. Many senior managers thought of the initiative as a way to give an indirect gift or a donation rather than as a serious program that would benefit both the rural communities and Thailand as a whole. As a result, TBIRD's first efforts were largely unsuccessful: In its first year of existence, it persuaded fewer than half a dozen companies to join the program.

In order to convince companies that the initiative would be worth their time and money, Mechai had to make the adoption—the process of working with the villagers—convenient and painless. Then he had to rethink the benefits of the effort and create some direct reward for the sponsoring companies. To accomplish those tasks, Mechai and his team developed a process that, among other things, took the following steps: First, TBIRD provided a personal adviser to each company that agreed to participate. Before the company got involved with the village, the adviser would provide a comprehensive assessment of the village's needs. As the program took shape, the adviser would act as a facilitator or mediator between the company and the village leaders. Second, TBIRD advisers would become residents of the designated village or villages until the program was well underway; they would help the company and the village select appropriate projects that would benefit both parties. For example, Bangkok Glass Industry Company, with the help of such an adviser, trained villagers to make brushes for cleaning its glass molds. The company set up a production facility to produce 150 brushes a day. Previously, Bangkok Glass had outsourced such work to other established companies; now it was paying villagers instead. Similarly, in a different village, Singer (Thailand) established a training school to teach young women to sew and followed up with a contract for 600 uniforms.

Slowly, TBIRD repositioned its campaign so that corporate sponsors were drawing direct benefits from their efforts. Equally important, TBIRD's new process made it easier for corporations to adopt the new behavior. The end result? Within two years of the program's reconfiguration, nearly 100 companies were in TBIRD's adoption pipeline.

For this social-marketing challenge, a highly moralistic campaign aimed at creating a sense of guilt in the target community—the area's companies—would have been a complete waste. Indeed, many social-marketing programs in Cell B fail because they take an overly moralistic tone and attempt to evangelize. The key to a Cell B challenge is information *backed up with convenience mechanisms*. A small proportion of a target audience may alter its behavior because of its convictions, but if a behavior change is made easy and if the campaign is persistent enough, even those who were unconvinced may switch.

Cell C

In Cell C, the individual benefits of a behavior change are clear, but the cost of such change is daunting. Social-change campaigns that fall into Cell C thus require a good deal of *push marketing* in addition to strong communication campaigns. In conventional marketing situations, push marketing can be thought of as what happens once a consumer has developed some broad general interest in a product or a service but has not yet decided on purchasing a specific brand. Before making a decision, the consumer may talk with friends or salespeople. He or she may read literature on the product, such as independent reviews or manufacturers' brochures. The consumer is also likely to be exposed to additional promotional material at the point of purchase.

In social-change efforts, push marketing consists of intensive support provided to the target community *at the community level*. Without that support, a Cell C campaign will not succeed. Unfortunately, although many social marketers realize the need for such support, Cell C initiatives are rarely balanced correctly. Many Cell C programs are hopelessly one-sided—they focus either on communication or on intensive support, not on a combination of both.

Consider the unsuccessful antidrug campaign mentioned in the introduction. Initially, it was weighted heavily on the side of communication through advertisements. One advertisement, typical of the sort the campaign used, featured teenage actress Nancy McKeon, who directly addressed viewers with an admonition that drug abuse is dangerous. The message was "Be cool like me. Don't do drugs."

Another ad that received a lot of airtime featured a slow-motion study of an adolescent girl. She is shown first taking drugs with her friends, then being wheeled on a gurney into a hospital emergency room. The soundtrack is the song "Take Me Out to the Ball Game," with the words changed as follows: "Take me out of the ball game;/Take me out of the crowd;/Buy me some pieces of crack, Jack;/I don't care if I never come back…." That ad ended with then-Mayor Raymond Flynn urging Boston's schoolchildren to reject drugs. A final example of the genre showed a teenage boy in his bedroom, obviously strung out on drugs. He addresses the viewer, saying that his parents are "dumb" and that they don't understand him and his need for help. At the ad's conclusion, a voice announces a toll-free hot line to use if a friend or child needs help for a drug problem.

The ads did have some effect: When Flynn commissioned a marketing research team to study the campaign's effects and offer advice on how to proceed, focus groups revealed that the city's school-age children had very high recognition of the antidrug public-service announcements. They could even recall several visual and written elements of the campaigns that had been aired frequently by local television stations, though they found the celebrity messages artificial. The children understood intellectually the harmful effects of drug abuse. Unfortunately, however, they felt unable to change any abusive behavior. The campaign had little or no influence on whether and how often the children took drugs.

The research revealed that many children took drugs because they wanted to be accepted by their peers. Saying no violated their social norms and network. To say no, they needed coping mechanisms. For example, they needed help inventing excuses not to take drugs, because they didn't want to say no outright. They also needed to know where to go to talk about drugs. The research found that parents and teachers were not a preferred outlet; the children felt more comfortable talking with counselors in community centers. In short, the research team concluded that an effective antidrug campaign would have to include not only information but also a strong support system for altered behavior.

Marketers with Cell C problems must go well beyond identifying their target community's behavior and communicating why change is desirable. In order for a Cell C campaign to have an effect, it must also address the context of the challenge. What external factors are influencing the target audience? Will the marketing campaign need to address those as well? If so, how much effort needs to be devoted to support mechanisms? What kinds of follow-up procedures are needed? With the Boston schoolchildren, only a concerted community-support program could insulate the children in the short run while educating them about the harmful consequences of drug abuse and giving them the strength to say no on their own.

Cell D

Displayed here are all the anomalies that make marketing social change so difficult. From the potential adopter's perspective, the cost-benefit ratio in a Cell D endeavor is terribly disadvantageous. The benefits are intangible in the short run and the cost of change is high.

The first thing marketers should do when they have a Cell D challenge on their hands is determine whether the initiative can be repositioned into Cell C. That is, they should try to figure out whether there is some way to show the target community a more direct benefit. Consider the Bangladesh family-planning example. After extensive research, Population Services International (PSI), a nonprofit organization based in Washington, D.C., concluded that although Bangladeshi men were unable to see the long-term economic benefits or quality-of-life considerations associated with family planning, women could. Women indicated that they were receptive to the concept of family planning as a way to improve their health and the health of their existing children. Women also saw that such planning would lead to opportunities for a better education, and, in general, a more prosperous existence. They did not have the same reservations about family planning that men had.

In theory, because the women could see a direct benefit from family planning, the campaign should have been easy to shift into Cell C. The marketers didn't have to design or build in new benefits. The target community as a whole could be persuaded to participate through the commitment of the women. But in practice, such a shift was difficult to accomplish. The marketers had to overcome a strong cultural barrier. In Bangladesh, the men usually did most of the household shopping. They did not generally discuss personal issues such as family size with their wives. And, in any case, women would be embarrassed to buy contraceptives in a public place. PSI's male contraceptives were being widely distributed, but for the family planning program to be truly effective, women had to become empowered consumers.

In order to reposition the program to Cell C, PSI launched a two-pronged effort. First, it made female contraceptives available through the country's 100,000 rural medical practitioners. RMPs participate in village community activities and are respected and regarded as friends, philosophers, and guides by many village people. And since RMPs make house calls, women would be spared the embarrassment of going out to buy contraceptives.

Second, and just as important, PSI mounted a new communication program directed at the men. The aim of that program was to break down cultural barriers and encourage men to discuss family planning issues with their wives. The program—which consisted, in part, of film ads shown at traveling cinema shows—did not seek to cause a cultural revolution by showing females in dominant, decision-making roles. Rather, it co-opted the men by portraying one of their peers discussing the subject with his wife and drawing the conclusion that he should be supportive of the idea.

Today, Bangladesh's family planning program is widely considered a success. In the 1980s, only 4% of targeted Bangladeshi couples practiced family planning. According to the Demographic and Health Survey of Bangladesh, that number has risen in the 1990s to 45%. Other informed sources estimate the number at 60%.

Of course, it is not always possible to move a Cell D project to another cell. If such a shift cannot be accomplished, social marketers first must try to persuade a small portion of the target community to change their behavior and then must leverage the power of those early adopters. As we have said, early adopters often stand to lose if the rest of the target group do not quickly accept and implement the behavior modification. But if a few participants become committed to the cause, it is in their best interest to become active agents for change. Marketers can use this motivation to great advantage if they are prepared to guide the early adopters' enthusiasm.

Think back to the producers of CFCs. The governments of the United States, Canada, Sweden, and Norway banned the use of CFC aerosols in the late 1970s. However, it was not until the mid-1980s, when it was proven that CFCs had indeed damaged the ozone layer, that the chemical companies themselves began to act as agents for social change. With their participation, the effort to eliminate CFC production gained serious momentum.

Until the mid-1980s, U.S., European, and Japanese companies continued to produce CFCs for non-aerosol applications. Each company knew that acting alone not only wouldn't solve the problem but also would put it at a severe disadvantage in the marketplace. Indeed, even a unilateral U.S. action would have disadvantaged about half a dozen U.S. chemical companies active in the global market. But with the United States accounting for nearly 50% of world CFC production and consumption, the U.S. companies, led by DuPont, realized that a consortium of chemical companies *could* influence the industry. As a result, in 1986, with the active support of U.S. CFC producers, the United States assumed a proactive stance in the United Nations Environmental Program (UNEP), which culminated in the Montreal Protocol of 1987—a landmark agreement that provides for a 50% cut from 1986 levels of CFC production by 1999.

The CFC war is not yet won. But there have been victories, in large part as a result of the ability of international institutions such as the UNEP to provide a forum in which countries can look for a way to protect the ozone layer without concomitant disadvantages for the chemical companies.

Supply-side persuasion—in this case, appealing to the manufacturers of CFCs rather than the consumers—is a viable approach to a Cell D challenge. But other, more indirect approaches can help a cause succeed over the long term as well. Moral persuasion, peer pressure, and demarketing activities aimed at the infrastructure supporting the supplier are effective tactics for both Cell C and Cell D challenges because they influence social and cultural attitudes. Consider the smoking cessation campaigns in the United States. The allure of smoking started to diminish as, one by one, social and cultural mores began to change. Gradually, smoking ceased to be seen as sexy, powerful, liberating, or a sign of success; instead, smokers began to be perceived as people needing help to kick a very bad habit. The burst of scientific evidence—including evidence of the harmful effects of passive smoking—and the response by federal, state, and local governments to those unequivocal data all served to fuel the antismoking movement. Smoking cessation campaigns, which were once perceived as an attempt to infringe on individual rights, are seen in the 1990s as informative, credible, and useful.

Mission Driven, Market Led

Correctly analyzing the nature of a social-marketing initiative can increase its chances of success, but there are several additional factors to reckon with.

Perhaps the greatest of these is the zeal of the marketers themselves. Many social-change organizations are founded and run by people extremely committed to and enthusiastic about the cause and mission of the organization. Usually they have undertaken personal sacrifices in order to work for a cause that is consistent with their values. But sometimes their enthusiasm overrides consideration of the real needs of the intended beneficiaries of their work. Ask the clients of public-service-advertisement campaign teams that donate their talent and time free to the cause. The clients will tell you that those wonderfully gifted teams often develop ads that convey the teams' vision instead of addressing the clients' needs.

Consider the dedication of the voluntary staff in one community center in Boston. Each staff member had his or her own ideas on how to persuade children to stop doing drugs. One pushed sports, another tried to educate children about the life-threatening consequences of drug abuse, and a third counseled the children simply to repudiate drug pushers. Although the research mentioned earlier showed that what the children needed was a way to say no to their peers, none of the counselors could offer them that kind of coping strategy.

Our framework urges social marketers to consider the costs and benefits of any given change effort from the viewpoint of the market—the target community. But therein lies another significant tension. Because social-marketing initiatives rely primarily on donors, volunteers, and other funding sources to support their operations, confusion can arise over whether and how much a social-marketing organization should also consider the opinions of its supporters. In order to succeed, social-marketing managers must make the wishes and needs of the various constituencies converge.

That challenge is further complicated by the fact that many social-change organizations lack good systems for measuring performance. Because the goal of the organization is not to enhance profits but to provide an often intangible and complex social good, managers often lack objective data with which to measure the success or failure of their programs.

In the face of such obstacles, social marketers must remain mission driven but market led. It is the only way that they can succeed. Their efforts must be guided first and foremost by a sensitive understanding of the target community. If the needs of the target community are addressed, the message will be more compelling, the means more efficient, and the mission ultimately more successful.

Originally published in May–June 1996. Reprint 96308

Note

The authors are grateful to Sanjay Bijawat for his many useful ideas concerning this manuscript.

AEI's President on Measuring the Impact of Ideas

by Arthur C. Brooks

IN THE SUMMER OF 2008 I was happily working as a professor at Syracuse University when I received an unexpected phone call. For the previous year the American Enterprise Institute—one of the oldest and best-known think tanks in the country, where I had a part-time affiliation—had been searching for a new president. Was I willing to be considered for the job?

The think-tank industry is very small, so it has no established pipeline for leadership. Boards are never exactly sure what type of people should lead these organizations, and executive searches frequently prove challenging. I happen to know I wasn't the first choice—or the second or third. For years I'd taught and written about fundraising and managing nonprofits, but I'd never actually practiced either. I'm convinced that the last thing AEI's directors said before offering me the job must have been "Ah, what the hell—let's give him a shot." But I got lucky. They made the offer. I accepted.

Working as a first-time chief executive is a challenging proposition on its face. But I faced more than just the standard learning curve: Between the time I accepted the position, in mid-2008, and when I started, the following January, the nonprofit economy imploded as a result of the Great Recession. Charitable giving in inflation-adjusted terms fell by almost 10% from 2008 to 2009, most of it during the last quarter of the year. AEI is fully dependent on charitable giving, accepting no government grants or contract research; thus its revenue plummeted just as I was walking in the door. The institute had to compete for every dollar as never before. My new colleagues and I had to show donors why their shrinking philanthropic investments should come to us rather than go to others, and how investment in our work would create tangible impact.

Even before the recession, demonstrating impact was a growing concern in the nonprofit sector. For-profit businesses can quantify their impact using metrics such as sales and shareholder returns, but nonprofits can't. That's doubly true for nonprofits in the world of pure ideas, like AEI. What is the metric for us—clever thoughts per hour? Yet modern philanthropists, many of whom have made vast fortunes in analytics-driven high-tech businesses, demand proof that their charitable dollars are doing real good. Mark Zuckerberg and others like him won't give to organizations that swallow up their money without producing measurable results. His generation insists on evidence that they're creating value with what they give. They need to see data. Having an intangible product is no excuse.

Show impact or fail—that was my initial major challenge as president of AEI. It led to plenty of sleepless nights in my first couple of years on the job. But meeting that challenge turned out to be more than a question of my personal survival in a new role. It has fundamentally changed how we do business.

A Golden Opportunity

To leave a tenured job for an uncertain future as a nonprofit manager may sound imprudent. It was actually of a piece with the behavioral patterns I had established up to that point in life.

I grew up in Seattle in a family of artists and academics. From a young age, I showed an aptitude for music, and I quickly found my way to the French horn. I gave college a shot after high school

Idea in Brief

After the Great Recession, the American Enterprise Institute, a Washington think tank, needed to compete even harder for every dollar. Arthur C. Brooks and his colleagues set out to demonstrate its true impact to a generation of data-savvy philanthropists.

AEI's *output* is pretty straightforward: books, research articles, op-eds, media appearances, and so on. Determining its *impact* meant measuring its competitive standing in the marketplace of ideas.

Brooks describes two of the metrics AEI uses: how many op-eds its scholars publish in prominent newspapers and how often those scholars are called by Congress to give testimony. Measured against its four leading competitors, AEI can claim 36% of op-eds over the period 2015–2017 and the most testimonies (by a wide margin) in the years 2009–2017.

but left after a year and set out with my horn to make a living as a classical and jazz musician in the United States and Europe.

A few years into my career as a musician, I met a girl from Barcelona and took a job with an orchestra in Spain in an attempt to persuade her to marry me. We had no common language when we met, but having recently celebrated our 26th anniversary, with three kids nearing adulthood, I'm pleased to report that our communications skills have improved since that time.

I loved being a musician, but it always bothered me that I'd never finished school, and that nagging sense only grew over time. So while still living in Spain, I restarted college via correspondence courses.

A month before my 30th birthday, I walked out to my mailbox and collected my bachelor's degree in economics. Not long after, I walked away from music entirely and returned to the U.S. to pursue a master's in economics, which led to a PhD in public policy analysis, which led to work as a university professor. I eventually landed at Syracuse.

During my decade in academia, I taught a lot of students from administration and MBA programs, and much of my research focused on nonprofit management and social entrepreneurship. I wrote a textbook on the subject. One of the central questions

I kept confronting was that of value creation: *How do nonprofits, except those that deliver the most tangible products or services, know they're creating real value?* The field, myself included, never seemed to have satisfactory answers. I'd talk a lot about "social return on investment" and "the double bottom line," but those were more theoretical concepts than practical, actionable guidelines. The move to AEI struck me as a golden opportunity to sort out these theoretical puzzles from within the real world of management.

But the decision to move to AEI was also deeply personal: I was a true believer in the organization's core principles. AEI is strictly nonpartisan, eschewing political entanglements and institutional positions. What unites the scholars and the staff is a shared commitment to a simple moral maxim: The free-enterprise system and American leadership in the world are pillars in the fight to defend human dignity against poverty and tyranny and to help lift up people on the margins. Learning about the amazing antipoverty record of global capitalism and free trade was a huge part of what had attracted me to the study of economics in the first place. Now I had the opportunity to dedicate all my work to sharing this truth with the world.

My deep admiration for AEI actually posed a bit of a problem. What if, as an inexperienced executive, I failed, hurting the organization in the process? When I was trying to decide whether to take the position, I had breakfast with Tully Friedman, the private equity pioneer and a longtime AEI board member who later became AEI's chairman and one of my closest friends. I worried aloud about what would happen if I failed in the job and imperiled this 75-year-old think tank. "Don't worry about that," he said. "If you can't raise money or motivate the scholars, we'll fire you within the year, and AEI will be just fine." This was oddly reassuring. So with a mix of excitement and panic, I tossed my tenure and made the move to Washington.

Not Outputs or Inputs but Impact

Nonprofit leaders typically make two mistakes when trying to answer the question "How do we know if we're having an impact?" The first is what I call the *sui generis* error. It's the idea that our work is unique and our organization is so unlike anything else that exists that we can't compare it with—or measure it against—any other organization. It's amazing how many smart people really believe this about their own organizations or those they love. It's a spurious claim, but I hear it all the time. And philanthropists hear it even more often.

The second mistake is the "lamppost error," named for the story about a guy who loses his keys in the street and spends hours looking for them under a lamppost because the light is better there. Nonprofits struggling to measure effectiveness will frequently turn to whatever is easiest to see—usually inputs such as how much they've received in contributions or outputs such as how busy they have been. This is obviously inadequate, because what we're really interested in isn't inputs or outputs but *impact*.

The *sui generis* error leads to not measuring anything, and the lamppost error leads to measuring the wrong things. My colleagues and I set out to avoid both pitfalls and create a better way to understand and describe our true progress.

AEI's output is pretty straightforward: books, research articles, op-eds, media appearances, public events, and so on. These products effectively constitute our supply curve. But nobody contends that simply writing an op-ed, publishing a peer-reviewed paper, or booking a scholar on television automatically guarantees a change in how leaders think and act. As a result, our output metrics are not particularly interesting in isolation. To move from output metrics to impact metrics, we had to overlay a demand curve on our supply curve. We had to find ways—even imperfect ways— of measuring how much leaders wanted and sought our work.

In the ideas industry this kind of demand is almost never directly observable. No matter how much excellent work a single organization may be doing to educate leaders or raise the profile of a given issue, no metric such as public opinion polls, election results, or legislative votes can show the organization's role amid the static of thousands of other variables.

Instead of *direct* impact measures, we realized, think tanks need to develop *proxy* impact measures, by searching for where their supply curve intersects with competitive demand in the market-place of ideas. We had to identify and track the products that leaders consume at some cost to themselves and in a direct trade-off with alternatives. In isolation, each of these metrics is a single point of limited utility. But considered together, they paint a pointillistic picture that helps us assess the impact of our work.

Here are just two examples from the suite of proxy metrics we've come to use:

The most prestigious national newspapers each receive about 1,000 unsolicited op-ed submissions every week. The "market" for real estate on those papers' opinion pages is unbelievably competitive, and editorial staffers ruthlessly reject everything except what they believe readers most need and want. That selectivity can reveal competitive demand for our product. Thus, although total op-eds written per year is just an output metric, the number of op-eds our scholars publish in a defined set of the most competitive outlets constitutes a viable proxy measure for impact. Though far from a catchall figure, this metric has one particularly useful aspect: The data is by definition public and thus allows comparison with peers and competitors. Every year to date, AEI has maintained a lead.

We do the same thing with congressional testimony. Most policy experts want to testify on the Hill, but they can't just call up the Senate switchboard and get on the docket. The Senate calls *you*. So although nobody believes that public testimonies are the only way think tanks shape the debate, they do offer one useful angle for measuring impact. And again, it is helpful that everyone's data is a matter of public record. When we initially analyzed these numbers, during the 110th Congress (2007–2009), AEI was in fourth place among think tanks in terms of congressional testimony. By the 111th Congress we were number one, and we've maintained that position ever since.

It's worth emphasizing again: Neither of these metrics is a direct measure of impact, let alone a perfect one. All such proxy metrics can be gamed or misunderstood, and each reveals only a partial dimension of the truth. And not all worthwhile proxy metrics can be used to compare competitors. For example, our scholars' personal relationships and private briefings with policy makers and journalists are prime proxy metrics of impact, because the leaders' time and attention is so scarce. But it is impossible to compare such proprietary data across organizations.

The point is not to search for one perfect proxy. Instead, nonprofits operating in the ideas industry can build a dashboard, outfit it with a wide variety of variables like these, and then use it to gauge the revealed preferences of public leaders and the uptake of the organization's work.

Clarifying the Mission

At the same time we began constructing this impact dashboard, my AEI management colleagues and I made several complementary changes. For example, we reworked how the organization talks about itself to better reflect our definition of success. Think-tank mission statements are more often uninspiring product lists ("We produce high-quality policy research") than true expressions of purpose. In consultation with our scholars and supporters, we wrote a new statement of purpose: "The American Enterprise Institute is a public policy think tank dedicated to defending human dignity, expanding human potential, and building a freer and safer world. The work of our scholars and staff advances ideas rooted in our belief in democracy, free enterprise, American strength and global leadership, solidarity with those at the periphery of our society, and a pluralistic, entrepreneurial culture." We tried to make clear the moral goal of our ideas, which is to serve others, especially those at the margins of society.

We then launched a series of high-profile entrepreneurial ventures expressly designed to create impact and fulfill our new statement of purpose. Some of them are quite unusual, such as research on happiness, experimental multimedia ventures, and a major collaboration with the Dalai Lama. Our newest venture in this series focuses on despair and human dignity in America. Its aim is to find and propose long-term solutions to the underlying causes of the social and economic despair that defined both sides in the most recent presidential

Measuring Impact

Op-Eds

Think-tank scholars write many op-eds, but that's a measure of output. To better understand its impact, AEI began tracking how many of its op-eds were published by three leading newspapers—the *New York Times*, the *Wall Street Journal,* and the *Washington Post*—and how its placements compared with those of competing think tanks over time. The percentages reflect yearly averages for the period 2015 to 2017.

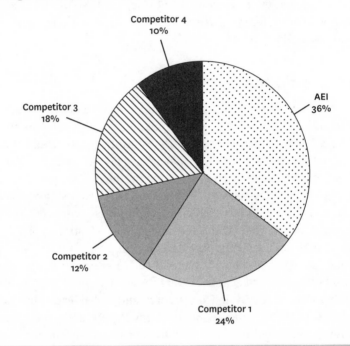

election. The program has four main pillars: vocational and technical training to help people find good jobs; using free enterprise to strengthen the economic security of families; reforming the criminal justice system; and finding new strategies to curb the epidemic of opioid abuse.

Built and marketed like an internal start-up, this venture does not displace any of our other work. To promote it to investors, we created a prospectus and a pitch deck, just as any start-up does. We approach

Congressional Testimonies

Testifying before congressional committees is another way AEI scholars can have real influence. When Arthur Brooks arrived and urged AEI to start gathering this data, the organization ranked fourth on this measure. Since then it has moved into the top slot, and its market share has grown.

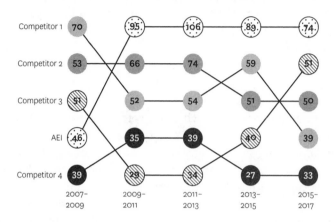

Source: (both charts) AEI
Note: Competitors selected are those that had testimony totals closest to AEI's during the past five congresses.

would-be donors as we would venture capitalists (which many of them are). We talk about the ROI and establish the basket of impact metrics that we will use to demonstrate success.

Our new focus on impact has also helped us refine our audience development and segmentation. We believe that in the marketplace of ideas, we can classify potential consumers of our products into four groups according to their receptivity to a given message: *true believers* (who already agree), *persuadables* (who are open to hearing from us), *hostiles* (who think our perspective is stupid or evil), and *apathetics* (who couldn't care less). We cross these four attitudinal groups with the five key demographic groups—policy makers, business leaders, the media, community leaders, and academics—that form our target audience. This gives us a 4 × 5 matrix and enables us to balance our strategies and offerings across these groups to maximize impact and more effectively serve our mission principles.

Our Strategy Paid Off

As you might expect, these changes weren't always easy to implement. I made plenty of mistakes along the way. Some colleagues complained that I was asking them to spend too much time and energy collecting data—and in some cases they were right. More than once, I fell prey to measuring the wrong thing entirely. For example, I became concerned when attendance at a series of live events started to trend down. But after a few months, someone pointed out that we'd begun live-streaming the events on the web, where they were getting a lot of traffic. This insight led to an even better metric, subscribers to events and original video programming on our YouTube channel—a measure by which AEI now leads the think-tank industry.

Despite a few hiccups, our strategy has paid off. Since 2008 AEI's operating revenues have averaged annual growth of roughly 10%; the institute bought and renovated a new headquarters in downtown Washington, DC; and we have grown from 140 full-time scholars and staff members to 220. More important, we've seen the impact of our research increase among policy makers and other leaders in dramatic ways. It's an exciting time at AEI.

Naturally, this growth necessitated changes to our management structure. Managers now have more authority and autonomy regarding internal administration, while my role has become increasingly outward-facing. These days I'm on the road about half the time, meeting with prospective investors and delivering 175 speeches a year about our work.

As I look back on my early days leading AEI, I am grateful for the scary exigencies that led to the changes we made. Because donors demanded evidence that our inherently amorphous products were having an impact, we learned to measure and demonstrate that. Given the imperative to spread the word about our work in a crowded marketplace, we made investments in our communications systems that will pay off for years to come. All in all, I got vivid proof that crisis is the mother of invention.

Other nonprofits are now asking about our systems, and several major foundations have asked our staff to help their other grantees adopt some of our practices. It's satisfying to see this. But most of all, I'm grateful to be able to help our fellow social enterprises increase the impact of their efforts in a world that needs them more than ever.

Originally published in March–April 2018. Reprint R1802A

An Interview with Michelle Bachelet

Michelle Bachelet *was as a young woman tortured and exiled by the Chilean government. She went on to become the country's first female president, in 2006. Trained as a pediatrician, an epidemiologist, and a military strategist, she also led Chile's ministries of health and defense. After her presidency she served as the executive director of UN Women. She was elected President for a second term in 2013.* **Interviewed by Katherine Bell**

HBR: *How did the horrific treatment of your family by the Pinochet regime affect your ideas about leadership?*

Bachelet: It reinforced the idea that we always need to fight against fundamentalism. There is no good and bad, no monopoly of one side or another. You need to ask yourself, Are people struggling for an idea or vision that is against the human drive, and what will be the cost? I'm not advising that you should compromise on everything and not make decisions. But you need to make them considering all factors, and to try to produce agreement.

How did organizing activists in exile prepare you to lead the government?

I have been organizing things since I was born—camping trips, picnics, music festivals. I was always proposing ideas and implementing them. Exile was a continuation of that. We did what we needed to do, what we thought should be done. That time opened my mind to different cultures, which in turn enriched my capacity to see through the eyes of others when I analyze issues. When you are a leader, it's very important to understand why other people do not think as you do.

You've tackled major reforms in every ministry or agency you've led, and you're doing that again, bringing several agencies together at the U.N. What do you think makes organizations willing and able to change?

There's always resistance to change in organizations that have been functioning for a long time. First of all, as a leader, you have to clearly establish the vision and objectives of the new organization. And then you ask yourself, Is this structure conducive to achieving those goals? If not, you have to identify the obstacles and define a new kind of architecture. Then you need to socialize this new point of view. You need people to be convinced that this is the way we have to do things. It's not a waste of time to have all the necessary meetings and communication. This is not an easy matter. You need time, persistence, and patience. You have to push hard all the way around.

You studied medicine and military strategy. What lessons did you take from those disciplines?

Medicine taught me to look as deep as possible, to try to understand the roots of a problem before proposing solutions. It taught me to consider all the different options and find a "medicine" that will really solve the problem and not just look like you solved it. And from my military studies I learned that when you make a decision, you not only have to make sure it is grounded in evidence, in good information and good arguments, but you also have to put yourself in the shoes of the people who will be impacted by the decision. At the same time, opportunity is essential. You can't lose momentum.

What do you think made you successful as the first woman defense minister and president in a conservative country?

Before I held those roles, I served as Chile's first female minister of health, but that was linked to the kind of activities women always perform. Everybody saw me working hard and speaking the truth. When I was appointed minister of defense, power was the issue. They saw I was in command. I had the knowledge, and I was very active—flying planes, riding on a tank. When I became president, my nonconfrontational way of working was important. I pulled people to the center, understanding that the system has to adjust to the people and not the contrary. That created a lot of credibility and helped us implement reforms.

You promised to and did appoint women to 50% of the positions in your cabinet. How did that turn out?

Parity was a principle not only in the cabinet but all over the government—it applied to all the politically appointed positions. I always asked for many names so that I could choose the best people on the basis of their CVs and their capacities and skills. In some areas, of course, we didn't have enough women and in other areas we had too few men. But if you looked at the whole government, we achieved parity. I think this is very important because a female president is not enough in terms of changing mind-set and culture. We needed to progress even faster in terms of how people were perceiving women.

What should women do to address the pay gap?

If you approach the problem individually, it's a very long way to go. It's very important that women organize with other women, and develop networks and new organizations if necessary, so that they can share experiences and learn from good practices and know that they are not alone. It's important for women to understand that this gap in opportunities is not a personal issue, it's a structural issue, and you need to make changes at a structural level. For that you need to show force, and so creating networks will help a lot. Also, try to bring aboard a lot of men who can really understand the importance of a better world for both women and men.

As a single mother, how did you manage your work and home schedules?

I am always trying to do everything perfectly, but of course I wasn't perfect. I did my best. I tried to be very well organized and teach the kids how to live in an environment where Mom is working a lot. I would cook for the whole week and put notes on the kitchen table explaining everything: what the kids have to do, and who to call in case of what, and, of course, I'd make sure that if it was necessary they could always reach me. It's not easy, but it can be done.

Chile suffered a massive earthquake in your last days of your first term. How did you handle that?

Everybody told me that you need to avoid the tendency to do as much as you can before you leave office because your time has ended and now is the time for the new people. But of course the last 16 days of my presidency I was completely dedicated to the earthquake and all its consequences, and I had to be involved until the last minute. That was not only my job but my duty.

Originally published in September 2011. Reprint R1109M

The New Work of the Nonprofit Board

by Barbara E. Taylor, Richard P. Chait, and
Thomas P. Holland

Editor's Note: The new work of the nonprofit board isn't new anymore—in fact it wasn't very new when the authors wrote this article in the mid-1990s. But the old ways can be deeply entrenched, and the best practices that Taylor, Chait, and Holland describe still haven't been universally adopted—the statistics in the sidebar "The Sorry State of Nonprofit Boards," drawn from a study done 20 years after this article appeared in HBR, prove that. Nevertheless, "old boards" can learn to do the new work, and this piece provides a road map for evolving from "a collection of high-powered people engaged in low-level activities" into a dynamic, goal-driven board focused on advancing the organization's mission, strategic priorities, and long-term welfare.

EFFECTIVE GOVERNANCE BY THE BOARD of a nonprofit organization is a rare and unnatural act. Only the most uncommon of nonprofit boards functions as it should by harnessing the collective efforts of accomplished individuals to advance the institution's mission and long-term welfare. A board's contribution is meant to be strategic, the joint product of talented people brought together to apply their knowledge and experience to the major challenges facing the institution.

What happens instead? Nonprofit boards are often little more than a collection of high-powered people engaged in low-level activities. Why? The reasons are myriad. Sometimes the board is stymied by a chief executive who fears a strong board and hoards information, seeking the board's approval at the last moment. Sometimes board members lack sufficient understanding of the work of the institution and avoid dealing with issues requiring specialized knowledge. Individual board members may not bring themselves fully to the task of governance, because board membership generally carries little personal accountability. And often the powerful individuals who make up the board are unpracticed in working as members of a team. No matter which cause predominates, nonprofit board members are often left feeling discouraged and underused, and the organization gains no benefit from their talents. The stakes remain low, the meetings process-driven, the outcomes ambiguous, and the deliberations insular. Many members doubt whether a board *can* have any real power or influence.

The key to improved performance is discovering and doing what we call the *new work* of the board. Trustees are interested in results. High-powered people lose energy when fed a steady diet of trivia. They may oblige management by discussing climate control for art exhibitions, the condition of old steam lines, or the design of a new logo, but they get charged up when searching for a new CEO, successfully completing a capital campaign, or developing and implementing a strategic plan. *New work* is another term for work that matters.

The new work has four basic characteristics. First, it concerns itself with crucial, do-or-die issues central to the institution's success. Second, it is driven by results that are linked to defined timetables. Third, it has clear measures of success. Finally, it requires the engagement of the organization's internal and external constituencies. The new work generates high levels of interest and demands broad participation and widespread support.

The New Work Requires New Practices

The new work defies the conventions that have regulated board behavior in the past. Whereas the customary work of a nonprofit board is limited to scrutinizing management, the new work requires

Idea in Brief

Too often, the board of a nonprofit organization is little more than a collection of high-powered people engaged in low-level activities. But that can change, the authors say, if trustees are willing to take on the *new work* of the board. When they perform the new work, a board's members can significantly advance the institution's mission and long-term welfare.

Doing the new work requires a board to engage in new practices. First the board must go beyond rubber-stamping management's proposals and find out what issues really matter to the institution. It can do that by making the CEO paint the big picture of the organization's strategic concerns, by understanding key stakeholders, by consulting experts, and by deciding what needs to be measured in order to judge the institution's performance.

Second, a board doing the new work must take action: the board must not only set policy but also work with management to implement it. Third, the board must go beyond strictly functional organization: the new work requires flexibility and encourages ad hoc arrangements. Finally, board meetings—where boards underperform most visibly—should be driven by goals, not by processes.

The authors give many examples of boards that have successfully embraced the new work. The stakes are high: if boards demonstrated that they can change effectively, the professional staff at the institutions they serve just may follow suit.

new rules of engagement and unorthodox ways of fulfilling a board's responsibilities. The pressures on most nonprofits today are too great for the old model to suffice. Nonprofit leaders can take the following steps to improve board practices:

Find out what matters

Traditionally, nonprofit boards and CEOs have agreed that management defines problems and recommends solutions. A board might refine management's proposals but rarely rejects any. Why? Few trustees know the industry or the institution well enough to do more, and those who do dread being labeled as meddlers or micromanagers. Board members sometimes are made to feel that asking a thorny question or advancing an alternative opinion is disloyal to the administration. A vote on an issue is a vote on the CEO. But how can a reactive, uninformed board know what opportunities the organization is missing? And how much damage must the organization sustain before the board realizes something is amiss?

To do the new work, trustees and management together must determine the important issues and the agenda of the organization. Trustees need to understand what the CEO sees as the critical issues. They also need to know what other stakeholders and industry experts think, because no chief executive knows enough to be a board's sole supplier of information and counsel. Knowledgeable trustees can help inform the CEO's judgment. They can also perform a useful function for the CEO by focusing the organization's attention on issues that are unpopular within it or that fall outside the staff's capabilities. In addition, the board can find out what matters by engaging in the following four sets of activities:

Make the CEO paint the big picture. The litmus test of the chief executive's leadership is not the ability to solve problems alone but the capacity to articulate key questions and guide a collaborative effort to formulate answers. As one member of a museum's board observes, "What I want most from the president are the big ideas." The CEO must be willing to share responsibility, and the board must be willing to follow the CEO's lead—and ask questions. "If you don't do that," says one college's trustee, "the board doesn't really have a clue about what is going on. When a problem arises and the CEO needs the trustees, they won't own the problem or be willing to help solve it."

The CEO should review the organization's foremost strategic challenges annually with the board. The board, for its part, must consider whether the CEO accurately targeted and defined the issues. This is a moment, maybe *the* moment, in which the board adds value. Together, the CEO and the board must agree on the institution's priorities and strategic direction. Those considerations, in turn, will shape the work of the board and its evaluation of the CEO.

The board of a college in the South has formalized this process successfully. At a retreat each January, the CEO and the trustees rank the most important challenges facing the institution. Then the board structures its committees to reflect those priorities. Last year, for example, the board concluded that marketing and technological infrastructure were its top concerns. The board formed task forces of trustees and constituents to study those issues, to specify the decisions the board would have to make during the coming year, and to clarify the board's needs for information and education. At the May board meeting, the task forces provided initial reports, and the board decided how to organize in order to pursue the issues. Trustees also developed measurable expectations for the president that were linked to the board's top concerns.

Get to know key stakeholders. Boards and CEOs have to know what matters to the constituents they serve. The interactions of the old work—which were mostly social events and show-and-tell sessions—will not do. The new work requires two-way communication. As a college president remarks, part of the reason for such communication is "to make the board vulnerable to constituents"—to make it accessible and accountable rather than insulated from the ordinary life of the institution. In that spirit, the boards of several colleges now meet routinely with leaders of student, faculty, and alumni bodies to explore matters of common concern.

Consider the example of a residential treatment center for children with emotional disabilities. When a major benefactor died, the center needed to find new sources of income. While interviewing leaders of social service organizations (a major source of referrals), several board members were shocked to discover that the center was seen as elitist and interested only in easy cases. In fact, many professionals referred the easy cases to less expensive care and assumed that the center would reject the difficult ones. Alarmed by these misperceptions, the trustees formed a task force to guide a public relations effort. The board expanded to include trustees with ties to sources of referrals and strengthened its relationships with other constituents through educational events and joint programming. "I want to make sure this board is never again so out of touch with its community," said the board's chair at the end of the process.

Close ties between the board and constituents unnerve CEOs who are determined to be the board's sole source of information and fear that direct communication between trustees and stakeholders will weaken time-honored lines of authority. That reaction puzzles board members; as one college trustee asks, "Why not have students talk to trustees? What's there to hide? These are our clients. I'm old enough and smart enough to know that some people just want to complain. Trustees are as qualified as the president to interpret the views they express. The closer I get to reality, the better I can sympathize with and help the CEO."

Consult experts. Many nonprofits are susceptible to competitive forces and to changes in public policy. Consider, for example, the impact on museums of cuts in funding by the National Endowment for the Arts, or the effect on hospitals of efforts to reform federally funded health care. Unless trustees understand the basic economics, demographics, and politics of the industry, boards will be hard pressed to separate the trivial from the significant and the good news from the bad. The new work requires learning about the industry from many sources.

One of those sources should be experts on the board itself. Although boards regularly recruit trustees with expertise in functional areas like finance, law, and marketing, the new work requires a board to have more than a few trustees with relevant professional expertise: physicians on a hospital's board, academics on a college's board, social workers on a clinic's board. Expert trustees can guide fellow board members through a foreign culture. For example, one Ivy League institution counted a former university president among its board members. At one point, he criticized his colleagues for second-guessing the administration's disciplining of a fraternity, saying, "I'd be furious if my board did this." The board backed off. And at a liberal arts college, a trustee who was a professor at another school helped educate the board about the complexities of measuring teaching quality and reallocating academic positions from departments with declining enrollments to those with growing demand. At the same time, he helped establish the board's credibility with the faculty.

Another source of knowledge is outside experts. They can help boards understand competition, client demographics, trends in government support, and public policy debates. For example, the board of a Protestant theological seminary faced with declining enrollment conferred with experts on professional education, the economics of religious education, and the demographics of its own denomination. The trustees learned that their denomination's population would continue to decline, further eroding financial support for the seminary and job opportunities for new ministers. On its current course, the institution would be bankrupt in a few years. The seminary decided to leverage the strength of its high-quality faculty by becoming a resource to the broader Protestant community, offering theological education to laypeople and continuing education for church workers and ministers, both on campus and in local churches.

Decide what needs to be measured. Corporate boards typically monitor a limited number of performance indicators. Those vital signs convey the company's overall condition and signal potential problems. Nonprofit boards often lack comparable data, largely because the trustees and the staff have never determined what matters most.

Together, the board and management should identify 10 to 12 critical indicators of success. For a college, that may mean scrutinizing its tuition discount (the average remission the institution gives to students as financial aid). For a museum, it may mean measuring its total return on endowment investments. For a hospital, the board may monitor occupancy rates. Distinctive strategies can suggest novel measures. A boarding school focusing on computer literacy monitored the ratio between students' dial-ups to the campus network and their phone calls from their dorm rooms for pizza delivery. A rising percentage of network calls meant that students were becoming more comfortable with new technology. Using comparable creativity, an orchestra with an aging subscriber base monitored ticket sales to single people in their twenties and thirties who had attended chamber music programs with wine and cheese receptions held afterward.

Graphic comparisons against projections, past performance, or industry norms focus a board's attention on crucial issues and remind trustees that the ultimate goal of the board is to influence those indicators in a positive way. As the CEO of a college in the Midwest says, "We have a set of key performance indicators, explicitly linked to the strategic plan, that are reviewed at every meeting. We even put them on a pocket-size card that trustees can carry around."

Act on what matters

In the world of the old work, the lines were clearly drawn: the board remained on the policy-setting side of the net, management on the implementation side, and so the game of governance was played. In the new work, the board and management are on the same side of the net as partners in both roles. The question is not, Is this an issue of policy or implementation? Rather, the question is, Is the issue at hand important or unimportant, central or peripheral?

Today few nonprofits can risk barring the CEO from policy development or divorcing the board from policy implementation. In a capital campaign, establishing priorities and goals is setting policy, identifying prospects and making calls is implementation. In the search for a new CEO, determining selection criteria is making policy, designing the procedure and conducting the interviews is implementation. In brief, most important matters cannot be subdivided neatly into policy or administration.

In many instances, implementation is far more consequential than formulation. For example, in face-to-face meetings, trustees of a Catholic women's college persuaded affluent older alumnae to support a new institutional focus on serving poor minority women from the inner city. The board of another college, troubled by the decline in students able to pay full tuition, selected three trustees to assist the administration with the design of a marketing strategy aimed at attracting more students able to pay.

In another case, a university owned a commercial radio station. The board questioned how the station fit in with the school's mission. After deciding with the president that the university could turn profits from the sale of the station to better educational use, the trustees negotiated the transaction. Afterward, the president exulted, "This was the board at its best." The board members knew more than the staff about the radio business and about selling a major asset, and they put that knowledge to use.

Involving trustees in policy implementation can be critically important during a crisis. In the aftermath of the scandal at the United Way of America (the CEO used more than a million dollars of United Way money for personal expenses), the board and CEO of one local chapter agreed that each of the trustees would interview five business leaders to learn what the chapter might do to improve community support for an upcoming campaign. The advice was consistent: admit that the national organization had blundered badly, stop all payments to the national headquarters until the charges were resolved, promise that all funds would remain in the community, allow donor-designated contributions, and promise that the board would issue a public report on allocations. The CEO and the trustees accepted those recommendations and inaugurated an intense public-relations effort that engaged every board member. In the end, the campaign was almost as successful as the previous year's and was substantially more successful than those of other chapters in the region. That would not have been the case had the board only set policy.

Organize around what matters
The board's new work must be organized to deal with the institution's priorities. That may seem self-evident, but boards often organize their work in functionally oriented committees (physical plant, finance, public relations) that channel trustees toward low-stakes operational decisions. For the new work to happen, substance must dictate structure. Committees, work groups, and task forces must mirror the institution's strategic priorities.

Teaching an Old Board New Work

Old Work

1. Management defines problems, assesses options, and proposes solutions. Board listens, learns, approves, and monitors.

2. Board sets policy, which management implements. Respective territories are sharply defined; there is little or no border traffic. Domains are decided by organization chart.

3. Structure of standing committees parallels administrative functions. Premium is on permanent structure, established routines. Members occupy functional niches. Board maintains busywork.

4. Board meetings are process driven. Protocol doesn't vary. Function follows form. Emphasis is on transmission of information and reports.

5. Board is a collection of stars. It recruits people with an eye to expertise and status. The CEO cultivates individual relationships and exploits each trustee's talents.

New Work

1. Board and management discover issues that matter, mutually determine the agenda, and solve problems together.

2. Board and management both set policy and implement it. Lines are blurred, borders open. Domains are decided by nature of issue at hand.

3. Structure of board mirrors institution's strategic priorities. Premium is on flexibility, ad hoc arrangements. Members occupy functional intersections. Board creates centers of action.

4. Board meetings are goal driven. Protocol varies with circumstances. Form follows function. Emphasis is on participation and action.

5. Board is a constellation. It recruits team members with an eye to personality and overall chemistry. Board cultivates group norms and collective capabilities of trustees.

For instance, a theological seminary replaced most of its operationally oriented committees with ones that reflected the major goals of the strategic plan: globalizing the curriculum, improving relations with local churches, and providing continuing education for the ministry. The committees included trustees and constituents. One result: on the recommendation of the committee on church relations, the seminary established a clearing-house to provide local churches with technical assistance in such areas as financial management, adult education, and church governance.

In another example, the board of a preeminent women's college has under active consideration the creation of four "councils" (business affairs, campus affairs, external affairs, and governance and board affairs) as umbrellas for clusters of standing committees. The council on campus affairs, for example, would oversee the activities and orchestrate the annual agendas of the student-life, admissions, and trustee-faculty relations committees, which would meet only as necessary. The council chairs would coordinate the annual agendas of the four councils and suggest strategic issues for in-depth discussion at board meetings.

Task forces that include constituents and nontrustee experts can tackle critical yet discrete matters such as outsourcing certain functions or installing a total quality management program. For example, the board of an independent day school appointed two task forces to explore accreditation issues with the appropriate state and federal agencies. The task forces gathered information about demographic trends, accreditation requirements, and possible legislation that would affect independent schools. At a special Saturday session, the task forces presented their findings, the board discussed whether to seek accreditation and whether to become more selective, *and* the task forces disbanded. The work had been done.

Such "tissue paper" task forces (use and discard) drive the board toward real-time results, multiply leadership opportunities, and prevent longtime members from dominating standing committees. As one college's trustee confesses, "Many of our standing committees don't really shape policy or identify needs. They're an empty ritual, a burden, not an asset. In contrast, task forces are very effective. For example, we're looking at the cost and shape of a marketing plan. A task force helped the board understand the problem and recommended directions. There was a material difference in the sense of ownership."

Focus meetings on what matters

Boards are boards only in meetings, and yet meetings are where boards underperform most visibly. Many trustees think that lack of time is the most significant barrier to a board's ability to perform the new work. In fact, the greater problem is the failure to determine what matters and to let that imperative drive the frequency, format, and duration of board and committee meetings. And if a board can meet only infrequently or for short periods, trustees should consider realistically what they can deliver. The chair, the CEO, and perhaps the executive committee should design each meeting by asking the questions, What is the purpose of this meeting? and How can we organize it to fulfill that purpose? Four common responses will help illustrate the point.

We need more background to make a decision. This answer calls for a discussion led by a moderator. Discussion sessions can engage and educate the entire board about issues facing the institution. The goal is to air views, invite questions, and consider alternatives—not to win an argument. No specific decision is on the table, and no votes are taken.

Consider the case of the college board that was generally concerned—but not sufficiently informed—about the interrelated issues of student quality, tuition charges, and financial aid. Each year, the finance committee, usually under pressure to balance the next year's budget, presented a tuition recommendation to the board. The process afforded no practical opportunity for the board to study the causes and effects of tuition increases. Last year, the board convened explicitly to learn more about the effect of tuition and financial aid decisions on enrollment and student quality, as well as on the bottom line. Subsequently, the board devised principles to govern the finance committee's recommendations for the following year. Those principles included the decision to hold institutionally funded financial aid to below 25% of overall tuition but to use grants to attract better students. The board also decided to increase average class size in order to free up resources to enhance learning partnerships, including student-faculty research projects.

At another university, each of the board's key committees appears once a year before the whole board for a half-day session to present information on a substantive issue or special area. For example, the finance committee led a board session to explain capital budgeting, deferred maintenance, and depreciation of assets. A task force on instructional technology that included faculty and students held a panel discussion to describe the state of the art across the nation and how technology was being used on their campus to transform the learning process. As a result of such sessions, reports the chair, "The whole board becomes more knowledgeable about the issues. The old bean counters on the finance committee now see other aspects of the institution."

We don't know what to do about a current problem. The new work, by definition, grapples with complicated issues that defy easy solutions. Trustees and management must be able to present multiple perspectives and develop solutions that reflect the group's best thinking. A meeting's design is critical to making that happen. Discussion must center on the explicit question at hand, such as, What should be our top three priorities for the capital campaign? or What specific steps can the board take to improve ties to the corporate community?

Small groups create a more comfortable environment for trustees to speak freely. Says one college board member, "I may have a comment worthy of 16 ears, but not one worthy of 60." Small groups provide venues for brainstorming, arenas where there are no dumb questions or insane ideas. A board member of a midwestern university explains, "Before we added small group discussions, all 50 trustees sat passively and listened to a few people impart information. The process was superficial, and substantive participation was limited to the executive committee. Small groups allow everyone to participate genuinely."

We face a crisis. In times of crisis, business-as-usual must be pushed aside to allow the board to concentrate on the matter at hand. Crises might include the loss of a major source of funding, the sudden departure or death of the CEO, the rise of a competitor, or even a split within the board itself.

Focus on the Constellation, Not the Stars

HISTORICALLY, THE PRACTICE OF most large, well-established nonprofits has been to recruit stars as board members. The assumption was that a collection of exceptional individuals would equal an exceptional board. The new work of the board cannot be done by a powerful inner circle. Instead, everyone must get involved. That will set off a chain reaction: the more trustees are involved in meaningful work, the more they will know; the more they know, the more they can contribute to the team; and the more they contribute to the team, the more likely the stars will form a constellation.

Too often, an executive committee makes all the important decisions and expects the rest of the board to comply. As one university trustee reports, "The executive committee is a little closed club of trustees who give lip service to inclusiveness but don't really practice it. It's nice, I know, to have all that control, but it's not good for the rest of the board." In those situations, trustees outside the loop of power lose interest.

To function as a team, board members need equal and timely access to information. Agendas, minutes, and background information from task force and committee meetings should be distributed to all trustees, and the board should use technology—conference calls and E-mail—to increase timely communication. Executive-committee meetings should be open to all members of the board, and board and committee chairs should be coached to invite reticent trustees to speak, as well as to avoid premature closure of debates.

Given the collaborative character of the new work, prospective trustees should understand that governance is a collective enterprise. They should realize that the board will expect more than attendance, participation, and financial support. The holy trinity of wealth, work, and wisdom (sometimes in just that order!) that has guided the selection of trustees in the past must be changed. Says one trustee of a college in the Midwest, "The operating

For example, a local Alzheimer's Association chapter lost a major grant in 1993 and had no immediate prospects for significant new funding. The chair called a special meeting of the board to discuss restructuring the chapter's services. A review of the mission statement reminded trustees of the organization's purpose; an examination of what it would mean to reengineer the organization helped open up discussion of key issues. By the end of the meeting, board members accepted responsibility for specific tasks to help manage the crisis: explaining the chapter's mission to potential sponsors in principle for selection was to add as many friends as you could, in the hope that some of them would turn out to be helpful. That's a poor approach."

A better approach is to engage potential trustees as members of a task force or a committee so that everyone can become better acquainted—a mutual tryout. Rather than extend an invitation to join the board based chiefly on a prospect's track record, arrange a conversation to explore the fit between the individual and the institution and its board. Some entrepreneurs, industrial captains, and self-employed professionals, for instance, are intolerant of the convoluted decision-making processes and dispersed powers characteristic of most nonprofits. Those individuals, however successful, are unlikely to be effective trustees. Board members should love the organization for what it is as well as for what they hope to make it.

The capacity for team play will be enhanced if new trustees are incorporated as swiftly as possible into the new work of the board. New recruits need to know of recent strategic decisions and current challenges. In addition, the board might accommodate the committee preferences of new trustees so that the rookies can play comfortable positions and thus gain self-confidence and respect from their peers.

A mentoring program that matches a seasoned trustee with a new trustee provides another way to foster fellowship and to engage newcomers faster. On one board, the pair are seated together for the first year so that the mentor can quietly explain the history of issues before the board, answer questions, decipher the board's unwritten rules, and debrief the new trustee after meetings. A more careful approach to the selection of trustees, combined with a mentoring program, can help a board form the constellation it needs to work at peak effectiveness.

the community, exploring the restructuring experiences of other chapters, and examining with staff the best ways to smooth the transition to a smaller, more tightly focused organization.

We need to deal with sensitive governance issues. Executive sessions without the CEO present open lines of communication among trustees. "We have an executive session after each board meeting," says one college trustee. "We feel free to bring up anything at all. This is a time for us to really ask questions and probe." Among the

The Sorry State of Nonprofit Boards

NONPROFIT DIRECTORS OFTEN FALL SHORT in terms of knowledge and experience, and their boards as a whole need more-rigorous planning and procedures. Those are among the conclusions of Stanford researchers who recently surveyed 924 nonprofit directors. Some specific findings:

Directors lack critical skills	27% Directors who say that fellow board members lack a strong understanding of the organization's mission and strategy	32% Directors who are not satisfied with the board's ability to evaluate the organization's performance
Boards lack formal processes	42% Boards without an audit committee	69% Boards without a succession plan for the CEO or the executive director
Fundraising is overemphasized	90% In organizations that require directors to fundraise, board members who say that task is at least as important as their other duties	42% In organizations that require directors to donate, boards with a "give or get" (donate or raise) minimum
Upheaval is common	69% Organizations that have experienced at least one serious governance problem in the past decade	23% Boards that have asked the executive director to leave or have faced his or her unexpected resignation

Source: "2015 Survey on Board of Directors of Nonprofit Organizations," by David F. Larcker, William F. Meehan III, Nicholas Donatiello, and Brian Tayan.

questions a board might entertain in an executive session are, Did we deal with important issues? How did the meeting go? Can we better serve the CEO? Differences of opinion among trustees or between the board and the CEO can be treated more candidly in an executive session. Says one board member of a women's college in the South, "If there are sensitive issues, the executive session gives us a chance to counsel one another."

These examples of the new work and new structures are far from exhaustive. Boards should experiment with different formats for different purposes. Use what works.

Leading the Way

Trustees protest regularly that artists, academics, physicians, and other professionals stubbornly resist change. Yet governing boards are among the least innovative, least flexible elements of many nonprofits. Boards are as reluctant to forsake committees as faculty members and physicians are to eliminate departments. Trustees resist varied formats for board meetings more than musicians resist novel formats for concerts. And board members oppose new membership criteria as strongly as teachers oppose nontraditional certification.

This hypocrisy was plain to the chair of a midwestern university's board. "It's tough for a group like this to be self-conscious. They're classic CEOs. They can tell stories about empowerment and team building, but that's not how they got where they are. They are uncomfortable with questions like How are we doing? and How should we improve? Most of our members are heavy into productivity. The board isn't hesitant to ask faculty and administrators to answer these questions. The board wants everyone else's time to be more efficient and effective, but the board should look for ways to improve, too."

Too often, trustees assume that organizational success proves that the board has performed well, even when there is little evidence that the board played a significant role, and even when staff members say privately that the success was achieved *despite* the board. "Most boards have the attitude," a trustee of a women's college notes, "that if it ain't broke, don't fix it, but I think it's better to fix it before it breaks." A sympathetic explanation for the reluctance of most boards to experiment with substantial governance reforms would be the trustees' desire to do no harm. A less charitable explanation would be the trustees' desire to do no work.

———

Moving to the new work takes work. As the CEO of a midwestern university recounted after the institution's board had changed, "It required getting people out of their little corners, the areas that they had learned and owned. They wanted to work on what they knew best and leave the rest to others. They had to rotate around and learn everything in order to govern the organization. They've moved from being just guardians of the physical plant, overseers of the administration, and suits with deep pockets."

Boards across the nonprofit sector are calling on institutions to change. As trustees demand evidence of productivity gains, efficient processes, and enhanced outcomes, they should model the behavior they seek in others. If boards demonstrate the capacity to discard shibboleths, dismantle old structures, and desert deeply ingrained modes of operation, the professional staff may follow suit. If the board does not do the new work, the trustees' hypocrisy will be blatant, and the value added by the board will be too meager to inspire organizational reform.

Originally published in September–October 1996. Reprint 96509

An Interview with Bill T. Jones

Bill T. Jones *revolutionized modern dance through the company he founded in 1982 with his partner Arnie Zane, who later died of AIDS-related lymphoma. He's since choreographed over 120 works (including the Broadway hit* Fela!*) and is the artistic director of New York Live Arts.* **Interviewed by Dana Lissy and Alison Beard**

HBR: *Where do you get the ideas for your performances?*

Jones: Some people say my work is about feelings that run smack into realities of economics, politics, and power. You build a foundation with questions—How do I express the conflicted feelings I have right now? How do I find the language? What has been done? What could be done? Who will the collaborators be? How are we going to crack open another way of doing it? How do we move? What will the environment and music be? Who is this for?—and then show diligence and bravery every day in the studio. There are a lot of people who think, "We know what Bill does." How do you get them to think again?

You've said that doubt "burns like fire" in you. How do you overcome it?

I'm depressive. Six years ago I didn't know if I had the stuff to stay alive. This was after a MacArthur grant and two Tony awards, but still everything was like sawdust. So what do you do? One way through is to keep working. Going to therapy is another. So is looking into the eyes of the people who love you. For me, that's the man I married, Bjorn [Amelan], as well as my associate artistic director, Janet Wong, who whenever I'm despairing, looks at me in a way that says, "Why are you indulging in this? It's not who you are. We have work to do." So doubt is fought by love and commitment to something bigger.

And I take it to be sacred doubt. I come from potato pickers, poor people. Why am I not a doctor or a stockbroker? Because when I discovered the magic of arms and legs and time and space and an audience being moved by someone going from there to there, suddenly that was my religion.

Many of your team members have been with you for years. How do you inspire such loyalty?

Considering how volatile and confrontational I can be, it's a wonder there's this corps of talented people around me. Some of it is luck, but I think it's also showing vulnerability. You've got to know how to say, "I made a mistake." People also forgive a lot when they know what you love. They might say, "This guy I work with is crazy. But there's something about him. He's so real." To stay around for almost 40 years in this field, you've got to have something past bravery. People recognize there's something authentic here, that I'm coming from someplace deeply committed and not cynical.

What's your leadership style?

I'm not a George Balanchine who walks in and says, "Now, dear, you do this, you do this," and, boom, it's genius. I come in and say, "I like this movement at the beginning. Let's work a while and see what you do with variations on that." You've got to have people you trust. With Janet, sometimes I just say, "Well, you know what has to be done. I'm dreaming about what I'm going to do tomorrow, but this is not finished, so you're going to do it, then I'll respectfully acknowledge and critique your work." When one has a problem—this comes from a social therapist named Freda Rosen—a good leader knows how to ask the right questions, listen carefully, and organize the answers the team gives back. On my good days, I relax and think, "You don't have to have all the answers or win this argument. What's the best idea on the table?" One thing about being an artist: The ego is ferocious. It's my company, my name. That's true, but it's not going to get done without these people. So I lead by throwing out: "How can we do this?" And when the time is right, I give that passionate embrace, that "Come on!" that "Free at last!"

that "Let's move!" The group doesn't need it every day. But at times they've got to feel like your heart is on the line.

When does your tough side come out?

Sometimes I get frustrated. But No Drama Obama has been a lesson to many people of my description. When you are a black man in a milieu that is primarily white, you've got to be really careful. You cannot afford to be written off as brutal, because the world wants to make you that anyway. So, you've got to learn how to be cool. When the demons come howling out, I suffer. But then I say, "That meltdown yesterday had less to do with you than with me. I felt inadequate." They say, "You felt inadequate?" and come a little closer, and when they're close, I ask, "What do you think we should do next?" With Janet and me together, we have a mom and pop. If I'm a terrible daddy—a fire-breathing dragon—they still have a female presence who is gentle but tough as nails, always on point, knows exactly what has to be done. It's a healthy, wholesome place to work, and you will leave knowing more than when you came in.

How do you find talent?

In a dance audition, you might have 450 women, 125 men looking for two parts. Which one in that cattle call can you not stop looking at? Not because they're cute or even the best in the room but because you feel like they have a hunger for the material they've been given to do. They're voracious, and they show you something in the work. I learned from masters of karate: They look for the freshest minds. You need the seasoned ones, too. But sometimes the idea from the new person, who you'd expect to just shut up, is the one that's gold. If you're asking about other kinds of talent, like an executive director, the answer is sometimes you have to make them, to find a bright person early in their career and give them a challenge.

What advice do you give people who aspire to lead an arts organization?

How are you with raising money? It seems like a crass question, but it's true. To make this model—a company that wants to support the experimental; a research and performance facility with 184 seats—viable, you've got to be beating the bushes. In the visual arts world, they can sell a painting, a sculpture, an installation piece, but with dance, what's the thing a rich person gets? You've got to find a way to connect with their sense of adventure and the notion of art-making as a participation in the world of ideas.

You choreographed two very successful Broadway shows. What were the benefits and challenges of joining that mainstream?

There was a time when I would have been embarrassed to say that I made a Broadway show. But with *Spring Awakening,* the director Michael Mayer said, "I've seen your work, and I think your aesthetic would really lend itself to this piece I'm making." So he was speaking my language. I thought, "I'll give a little time to it. If it doesn't work I'll walk away." Then, of course, you get invested. With *Fela!,* the producer Stephen Hendel thought Broadway needed this new music and wanted a director that didn't come from that world. He believed in me and indulged me with five weeks of previews. So I was taken care of. I'm working on another show right now with a very experienced producer, who said, "We've got to work together." Broadway's a very conservative place, but I hold out hope that I can still contribute—and maybe it will be the cash cow that helps me retire.

Do you think about retirement and who might eventually succeed you? It's hard when your name's on it, isn't it?

Janet Wong is the first associate artistic director. Does she want to keep this thing? I don't know, but I think she loves it. One thing we're doing with New York Live Arts is figuring out how to use the Bill T. Jones brand—the vision, the practice, the dream, the legacy. It's the foundation, not the end.

What have been your biggest career turning points?

Going from being a young soloist to working with Arnie and having that relationship mature in public. Then Arnie, when he was dying, he said to me, "Why don't you just let the company go and do your solo thing?" and I decided, "No, this is our child, so I will do what I have to do and find the collaborators to keep it going."

How do you deal with grief?

Identify the qualities in the person that you lost and cultivate them in yourself; that way, you keep them alive. Also Janet coming into the company. She and I met at a gala. I was ranting about how hard this business is, how people don't have faith, and she came up to me and quietly said, "I have faith." That was 23 years ago. She meant it. Oh, and my retiring from performances—deciding that I was no longer going to be in my sweat clothes in the studio. The last full evening solo work that I did was at the Louvre, in Paris. It was a very special thing. But I had knee and back problems, and I decided to stop dancing. Of course, I still dance when I'm very happy or moved—sometimes in the living room, when guests are over, or at the end of a run by the company that's had a special energy. In fact, I'm performing my first solo commission in eight years on stage this season. It's an interesting problem to make it physically low-impact but with deep feeling.

Originally published in November 2015. Reprint R1511M

Reaching the Rich World's Poorest Consumers

by Muhammad Yunus, Frédéric Dalsace, David Menascé, and Bénédicte Faivre-Tavignot

POVERTY IS NOT JUST AN emerging-market problem. In the United States more than 45 million people, or 15% of the population, are officially poor, according to the Census Bureau. What's more, this percentage has increased every year but one (2006) since the 21st century began. At 16%, Japan is doing no better. And in the European Union almost 120 million people—one in every four—are classified as at risk of poverty or social exclusion.

In the past, businesses in the developed world have largely ignored the needs of these groups. To be sure, they know that not all their customers are rich, and many companies have invested significantly in creating low-cost products and services specifically tailored to people on a tight budget. Most automakers have offered low-budget cars for decades: The Model T Ford, the VW Beetle, the Mini Cooper, and the Citroën 2CV were in their time designed for what their manufacturers saw as the budget market. Low-cost "hard discounters" such as Aldi and Lidl in Europe and Market Basket in the United States have emerged relatively recently in the retail industry.

But the low-cost, low-price products and services that have traditionally served poorer consumers in Europe are usually still out of reach for the 25% who are at risk of poverty. Consumers in this group often can't buy essential products and services without significant aid from the state—whose ability to provide such aid is diminishing even as the need for it grows. Limited public transportation, for example, means that many poor people in rural districts must rely on aging, extremely cheap vehicles. Someone whose car breaks down may be out of work as a result.

In recent years a number of large corporations have started approaching problems of this kind in a new way. In 2009 Martin Hirsch, the former French high commissioner in charge of poverty alleviation, and Emmanuel Faber, then the food giant Danone's deputy general manager (now its CEO), came together to form the Action Tank—a not-for-profit association directed by Jacques Berger, of HEC. Through the Action Tank a number of leading multinationals have joined forces with NGOs and government organizations to experiment with developing social businesses in France.

"Social business" is a concept originally developed in the context of poor countries. Such a business has three key characteristics: First, it seeks to alleviate social problems, including all forms of poverty. Second, it must be run sustainably—that is, it should not lose money. Third, profits—when they exist—are reinvested in the business rather than funneled back to shareholders. Investors eventually get back only the money they initially invested. Danone and a growing number of other multinationals have for some time been engaged in social businesses in Bangladesh and other poor countries, but applications in the developed world are rare.

Among the first companies to join Danone in the Action Tank were the eye-care company Essilor, the construction giant Bouygues, the telecommunications group SFR, and the carmaker Renault. Early results from these companies' experiments suggest that the social business model is both an efficient way of fighting poverty and a productive source of new business ideas. Their ventures are sustainably

Idea in Brief

The Problem

Poverty reaches far beyond emerging markets. In the European Union alone, almost 120 million people—nearly 25% of the population—are deemed at risk of poverty or social exclusion.

The Current Approach

Corporations usually try to meet the needs of poorer consumers with low-cost, low-price offers while still making a profit. They have improved access to many products and services, but a substantial number of consumers are still largely excluded.

The Solution

In France, the not-for-profit Action Tank is experimenting with an alternative: the social business model. It differs in a number of ways from traditional low-cost models—beginning with the fact that its primary goal is to solve social problems for customers.

providing high-quality products and services to very poor people at rock-bottom prices.

Essilor's social business, Optique Solidaire, is a good example. Working with all the company's supply chain partners, including insurance companies, it has succeeded in driving down the cost of a pair of high-quality reading glasses to poor pensioners from 230–300 euros to less than 30 euros. After spending 15 months working out the offering and three months conducting an experiment in Marseille, Optique Solidaire has built a network of more than 500 "solidarity retailers" across France. They are opticians who have volunteered to spend some of their time selling the glasses at a sharply reduced profit margin. Target customers—people over 60 with minimal resources—receive a voucher and a letter from their insurance company telling them about the offer and supplying the address of the closest participating optician. Essilor's goal is to recruit 1,000 retailers in France and to equip 250,000 to 300,000 people with glasses they could not otherwise afford.

In the following pages we present the social business model that is emerging from experiments like this and demonstrate how radically it differs from traditional low-cost business models. The new model, perhaps counterintuitively, looks more like that of a high-end solutions provider than that of a discount supplier. Obviously, financial profit is not its goal. We will describe the business benefits, both tangible and intangible, that social businesses can provide and the factors that contribute most to their success.

The Model

Let's begin by looking at the value propositions that social business models offer. These typically involve:

Customer exclusivity

Unlike low-cost models, social business models are exclusive: Companies determine up front which and how many consumers the program will serve, and no one else is eligible for the offer. The target may be broad. For instance, SFR and the French charity Emmaüs, which focuses on the homeless, regard all poor people who have a mobile phone as eligible for the services offered through their project Téléphonie Solidaire. But the target may also be narrow, such as poor consumers older than 60 (Essilor), poor families with a child aged six months to 24 months (Danone), or poor consumers who need a car to get—or keep—a job (Renault).

In determining eligibility, social businesses usually work with nonprofits, which rely in turn on local associations and public programs to find potential beneficiaries. This approach also reduces companies' costs.

High-quality products and services

In a low-cost business model, every consumer, whether poor or not, evaluates the trade-off between the company's standard and low-cost offers. If they are too similar, the company runs the risk of cannibalizing its standard offer. Thus it must downgrade key attributes in the cheaper offer to create a distinct trade-off.

In a social business model, the offer can remain unchanged if the economics allow. This is important, because the goal of the social business is precisely to give poor people access to an *existing* product or service whenever possible. Danone, Renault, and SFR provide poor customers with products and services identical to those offered to richer ones. The only difference in Optique Solidaire's offering is a limited assortment of frames; lens quality remains the same.

The commitment to high quality means that social businesses don't lower their costs by redesigning products or manufacturing processes, as low-cost businesses may do. They focus on changing the economics of sales and distribution. The solution is often to partner with nonprofits or to work with distributors on a noncommercial basis, as Essilor did. And as we'll see, companies that devise an integrated, solution-style offering can offset costs in one component with savings in other components.

Carefully designed solutions

Unlike low-cost companies, which are defined largely in terms of products and services, a social business often (though not always) expresses its value proposition as a solution to a social problem customers have. Renault's Mobiliz is a case in point. The project's goal is to resolve transportation issues for poor people. In cities, Mobiliz works with the NGO Wimoov to find the cheapest form of mobility for working poor people, whether it be the metro, buses, or bicycles. In rural areas, however, the project's customers need access to a cheap car and affordable maintenance, which Mobiliz provides through a network of "solidarity garages." Network participants (garages owned or franchised by Renault) dedicate a portion of their time and resources to repairing damaged or broken cars for qualifying customers at a nominal cost. The French NGOs Wimoov, FASTT, and UDAF are responsible for "recruiting" customers.

An often-important part of social business solutions is promoting behavior change on the part of customers. Danone's Projet Malin, a joint program with the French Red Cross, provides low-income parents with affordable and nutritious food for children, educational materials, and courses delivered by independent third parties. "The purpose of our program is to ensure that children are well nourished," says Benjamin Cavalli, of the Red Cross. "We ask the mothers if they want to attend an educational workshop to develop good nutritional practices. Many do." (Programs must take care not to seem patronizing; for example, there's no need to lecture poor commuters on how to travel.)

Thinking in terms of solutions can help companies with the challenge of costs. Since 2000, French law has required that a city of more than 3,500 inhabitants that is part of an "urban center" of more than 50,000 must have at least 25% of its dwellings qualify as social (public) housing. Understandably, companies doing this kind of construction try to minimize direct costs through efficiency. But Bouygues realized that building apartments inexpensively didn't necessarily make them affordable over the long term.

Working with the Action Tank, the company estimated that in the Paris area, construction accounts for less than 30% of total housing costs over the life of a building. Land accounts for about 12%, financing for 15%, maintenance and repair for 12%, and usage (heat, electricity, water, garbage collection, and other running expenses) for about 35%. So the company has broadened its scope to offer a more integrated service. It has proposed innovations such as decreasing the size of individual units in order to build in neighborhoods with better connections to public transportation (an idea borrowed from the hotel industry), creating a common laundry room (unusual in France), asking tenants to take care of the cleaning (including the garbage), and setting up efficient water distribution systems. Some of these innovations would entail up-front costs, but the downstream savings would more than cover them.

The Hidden Payoffs

The primary purpose of a low-cost business is to create shareholder value by generating profits. Although the business makes products accessible to poor consumers, that is merely a means of delivering on its promise to shareholders. Because a social business seeks to alleviate social problems sustainably, however, its profits are plowed back into the company. But that's not to say that social businesses yield only social returns. In fact, the spillover effects of creating them may in the long run be as commercially valuable as the profits of a low-cost business. Those effects include uncovering opportunities for innovation in new markets, motivating employees, and enhancing the company's reputation—along with demand for its products and services.

Breakthrough innovation

Social businesses have long been recognized as what Rosabeth Moss Kanter, of Harvard Business School, has called "beta sites for innovation." Emmanuel Faber has described Danone's social business in Bangladesh, which started in 2005, as "the best R&D lab ever." To be sure, low-cost businesses do often trigger innovation in processes and design, but the innovation of social businesses tends to be more radical, because they are trying to maintain the original quality of their products and services. As we saw with Bouygues, this forces them to break away from product-centered innovation and focus instead on *consumer-centered* innovation.

François Rouvier, the manager of Mobiliz, says, "Developing the Dacia [Renault's low-cost car in Europe] was a formidable challenge for Renault. We started with existing cars and left no stone unturned to make it cheaper. In a sense, we were going downward. But in the social business model we put the constrained customer, not the product, at the center of the action, and we seek to help her go upward. This is a whole new mindset."

As a result, companies can identify ways to increase access to their commercial products as well. For example, Renault's consumer-centered research revealed that the prohibitive cost of qualifying for a driver's license was a major reason that fewer and fewer young people in France were buying cars. The company teamed up with ECF, France's leading driving school, to develop a computer game for learners. By speeding up the learning process, it can drastically cut the overall cost of lessons.

Social business models also spark innovation through the high level of collaboration they involve. In particular, they enable companies to leverage existing capabilities in the not-for-profit sector. Essilor has launched several commercial projects as a result of its experiment. In Southeast Asia, for example, it has applied the idea of sending vouchers to customers via a third party. Rather than waiting for people to visit opticians and buy glasses from them, Essilor works with corporations that send letters to their employees offering to share or even bear the cost of glasses. This improves both employees' quality of life and the quality of their work—a triple win that benefits Essilor, its customers, and their employers.

Motivation

Our experience shows that social business models generate a lot of motivation and meaning for workers, who are often less engaged when their employer's sole purpose is to make shareholders happy. One of Renault's goals for Mobiliz was to strengthen the social DNA of the company; the name stands for both the mobility of the consumers Renault serves and the mobilization of its people. The company has been surprised by how positively its dealer network and sales force have reacted.

"We thought Mobiliz would not be welcome, because by definition the model makes it impossible to make money," says Claire Martin, Renault's vice president for corporate social responsibility. "But we received encouragement from people throughout the firm. The reaction of the sales department was so favorable that we are now facing a highly unexpected problem: too many garages that volunteer and not enough low-income car owners who can be identified and channeled through our partnering NGOs." This level of enthusiasm almost certainly translates into higher rates of employee retention and productivity.

Reputation

Large corporations that introduce low-cost products are quickly suspected of trying to make money on the backs of the poor, which can damage their overall brand image. For instance, after Danone introduced low-cost yogurts on the French market in 2010, public reaction forced the company to discontinue the product line. Nutriset, the world leader in emergency food for developing countries, had to abandon two consecutive attempts to sell nutrition bars to very low income consumers in France, because social activists argued that it

How social businesses differ from low-cost businesses

Here's a quick comparison of the two models:

	Low-cost	Social
VALUE PROPOSITION	**Objective** To make a profit by improving access to products and services	To improve access to essential products and services in a financially sustainable manner
	Exclusivity Any consumer can buy the offer	The company decides who the targets are and how to filter them
	Quality Lower, to avoid cannibalizing the regular offer	Unchanged
	Focus Low-price products and services	Affordable solutions to social problems
SOURCE OF VALUE	**Operations** Reconfiguring the production supply chain to reduce costs	Reconfiguring the distribution supply chain to reach targeted consumers
	Partnerships Optional co-creation with profit-maximizing organizations	Required co-creation with third parties that have a social welfare objective
	Innovation Product-centered	Customer-centered and ecosystemic
	Employee motivation Weak	Strong
	Reputation May be quite low	Likely to be high

was an immoral way to make money and that the goal should be to offer "real meals."

But when a company starts a social business, which is expressly not for profit, it can change stakeholders' perceptions. The model breaks down barriers and helps the company build new relationships based on trust. Emmanuelle Vignaud, Danone's brand marketing manager, says, "Social business projects show that our firm has a more comprehensive and long-term mindset. We are not considered 'predators' anymore, which has concrete consequences. One key pediatrician, who had refused to meet with us before, agreed to be interviewed for more than two hours to help us understand how baby food will evolve. We have also earned the trust of two pediatricians' union leaders, who are involved on the board of Projet Malin. These relationships could be immensely useful as we look for new product ideas going forward."

To be sure, the low-cost model has a long history—probably best exemplified by the Model T Ford—of providing people with access to goods and services. Its ability to generate financial returns aligns it with the goals of most companies. We believe, however, that the social business model has the potential to provide even greater access, and its spillover benefits can create value over the long term, making it a significant alternative to low-cost business ventures.

Making the Model Work

Veolia, Total, La Poste, and Michelin are among the large organizations that are now joining the Action Tank to experiment with social businesses. The success of such projects in France has spurred the creation of action tanks in Portugal and Belgium to help companies develop similar programs. Our experience in France has enabled us to pinpoint the crucial factors.

Always put the social goal first

Companies must keep in mind the point we made earlier: Social businesses have *social goals* and *business spillovers,* not the reverse. If a social business is created to stimulate innovation or improve reputation, it will generate suspicion among its partners, threaten the cooperation needed for innovation, and look like corporate hypocrisy to company employees. This doesn't mean, of course, that you can't talk about the spillover effects—just that they have to take second place or you won't get them at all.

Be patient and selective in partnering

It takes time to construct the right model for the social problem you are addressing. (Schneider Electric has worked with the Action Tank since the latter's inception, but because it's primarily a B2B firm, selecting a project was challenging. Schneider is only now starting to experiment with measuring energy consumption for poor people.) Negotiations are necessary both internally and with external ecosystem partners. Finding the right organizations to partner with is difficult: You need to understand their cultures and mindsets—especially when they're non-profits, whose participation and credibility are essential for success. The Action Tank has been helpful in making connections and deepening understanding of partnership challenges, and many of the world's top consultancies have practices that specialize in social ventures.

Keep it as simple as you can

Poor people in developed countries often have a lot of choice. SFR and Emmaüs have identified more than 300 social service programs in France. But each has its own, sometimes complicated, processes and eligibility criteria, and poor people with limited time find it hard to make an informed choice among them. Even when a social business can identify all potential beneficiaries (as Optique Solidaire was able to), it's generally able to reach only about 30% of them. Some social businesses are now developing traditional push marketing initiatives such as advertising and couponing to raise public awareness of their products and services.

Start local

Don't try to launch a national program from scratch. Figuring out how to collaborate with nonprofits is better handled on a small scale. Luckily, the customer exclusivity of social businesses makes it easy to run experiments. Essilor needed 18 months to work out the right model including its pilot project in Marseille, and Danone's Projet Malin is still being refined in just four cities. Determining how to filter customers can be especially challenging.

Social business is still in its infancy. Early evidence suggests, however, that it can help companies looking for market-based solutions to poverty issues. Its business spillovers—innovation, motivation, and reputation—are significant. More important, it is demonstrating that large corporations can be powerful agents of social change when they partner with other organizations. And social businesses can unify all society's organizations, including businesses, nonprofits, and government agencies. That is no small achievement, because we need all our talents in the fight against poverty.

Originally published in March 2015. Reprint R1503B

An Interview with Muhammad Yunus

Muhammad Yunus *won a Nobel Peace Prize for spreading the concept of microcredit—tiny loans to help poor people start businesses—via his Bangladesh-based Grameen Bank.* **Interviewed by Alison Beard**

Microfinance has come under fire in recent years. How do you maintain quality control as your organization and your ideas spread?

The problem is not microcredit. It's using the idea for the wrong purposes. Some programs in India treated microcredit as an opportunity to make money. They blew it up and went to the stock market to float IPOs and so on. And that created all the tension. Now in some places even the loan sharks call their services microcredit. But we have no problem at Grameen Bank in Bangladesh, because microcredit has remained mission-driven. We want to help poor people. We don't see them as an object for making money.

How do you make sure all your people are adhering to the mission?

We have 2,600 branches at Grameen Bank. Each one is almost autonomous. But our goals are very clearly stated, and we monitor whether the branches are meeting them through something called Five Star. Each employee is supposed to look after 600 borrowers. If you get 100% repayment from those borrowers, you get a star. If the whole branch achieves 100%, then everyone in the branch gets a star. If you do it for the whole year, you get another star. If your branch is profitable, you get a fourth star. And if the children of the borrowers in your branch are all in school—every single child—you get the fifth star. These are stars you can wear on your chest, like in the military. So you go to work, and you see the star achievement.

What qualities do you look for in Grameen employees?

In the beginning, we were very small, so we were picky. We were trying to get the best possible staff. Now that we're hiring so many people, we're not looking for the ideal. There will be qualitative differences in the people we hire, but it's OK. Bring them in, and let them go through the process. We take many kinds of people, and the system turns them into ideal people.

Grameen Bank started out as a field research project. Why is getting out into the field so important?

When I was doing my PhD and then teaching, I developed a bird's-eye view. I could see a very wide spectrum of things, almost the whole world. But I was seeing only the outline of things and filling them in, like a child coloring in a box, by making up stories about how people behave. Then, working in the village, door-to-door, person-to-person, I got a worm's-eye view. I saw things at very close range—all the details, what really happens inside. And that's more important, because I could then clearly see what the problem was and try to solve it—to start with a tiny little problem, and feel energized by it.

How do you zoom out again?

I don't. I look just at one plot, not the whole plantation. I do the plot and it works, so I do the next plot the same way. You start with 100 people and then move to the next 100 people, and eventually you see you can simultaneously add 100 people here, another 100 people there and there. You're adding up to a bigger scale at a gradual speed. Then you have to monitor and start linking the structure and so on. But you're not designing at the outset for a million people, starting with a megastructure. You're moving step by step.

Still, you're also known for setting huge goals. Why do you do that?

I believe that if you put all the creative power of human beings on one side and all the problems of the world on the other, and put them into a battle, human creative power will always win. It's just that we don't use our creative power to address problems; we use it to make money. We have created a system of money-chasing entities, rather than problem-solving entities. So how do we break from this? Social business. Create companies that are devoted to solving a tiny slice of our problems and that operate with the efficiency of business—but whose investors don't expect any dividend. Making money is a happiness. Making other people happy is also a happiness. So why don't we do both and maximize our happiness?

Should every company be a social business, or have a part of it that's a social business?

Every company is a legal personality, so just as every person can do both, every company can do both. It's a choice, whether it's exclusively one or the other, or mixed in various proportions: 80/20 or 20/80. I'm not opposed to money-making. But why don't you create a tiny little social business on the side to take five people out of the welfare system, or provide health care or technology to a group without it, or create a business to employ juvenile delinquents? Whatever you feel comfortable with.

In the joint ventures you've done with big corporations, what are some of the obstacles you've faced?

I have more excitements than problems. But there was one interesting problem with Danone that became a classic case. We had a 50-50 joint venture agreement: Grameen would give €500,000, and so would Danone. Grameen had no problem. But Danone couldn't provide its half. Weeks went by, and they could not. Months went by; they could not. Finally, they explained. Their lawyers were objecting, saying that the money belonged to the shareholders and therefore couldn't be used to invest in a company that would not pay them a dividend. But then Danone came up with a solution. It sent out a letter to all the shareholders before the annual general meeting saying: We want to start a company in Bangladesh that will tackle the problem of malnourished children. If you want to use part of your dividend to invest in this company, please sign up and tell us what percentage you want to put in. Around 97% or 98% of the shareholders signed up, and Danone ended up with €35 million. So there was a problem, and there was a solution.

How hands-on is your role in Grameen's joint ventures?

I'm only one person. Most of the time, I'm not contributing personally in the design of the products. But I'm a catalyst for bringing people together, focusing on objectives, reminding everyone what we want. For example, in the Danone case, they first showed me a plastic container for yogurt. I said, "In social business, plastic is not allowed. We want biodegradable material." The Danone guys said, "We use plastic all over the world." And I said, "All over the world you're a profit maker. Here you're a social business." They were unhappy, but they started looking for a solution. After four months, they came back with a new container made of cornstarch. "Can I eat it?" I asked. "Because why should poor people spend money on something they have to throw away? Why can't you put nutrition in the cup?" So they worked very hard to make an edible cup. These big companies have enormous creative power. But unless you ask, you'll never get an answer.

You have such a wide network of supporters. How do you go about building those relationships and lobbying for your ideas?

I don't lobby for support. People become supporters because it matches their own wishes and desires to help the poor.

Fully 97% of Grameen's loans are to women. Are women better businesspeople than men?

Women used to hold less than 1% of bank loans in Bangladesh. So when I created Grameen, I wanted to make sure that half of the borrowers were women. When we approached them, they said, "I don't know what to do with money. I'm afraid of money. Give it to my husband." And I thought, "This is not the voice of the woman. This is the voice of history, of the system, which created fear in their minds." It took us six years to finally achieve the goal of 50/50. Then we saw that the women borrowers brought so much more benefit to their families. Women want to build up something for the future with their money. Men want to spend it enjoying themselves. So we changed our policy to focus on women.

Grameen works across the world now. What cultural differences have you seen?

We have a bank in New York City now—9,000 borrowers, an average loan of $1,500, repayment rate over 99%—and it's doing exactly the same things we do in Bangladesh. There is no cultural variation. We focus on what Grameen is: tiny loans to poor women.

Do you think you'll ever fully retire?

I don't think any human being wants to retire as long as they enjoy the life. And I'm enjoying the life.

Originally published in December 2012. Reprint R1212M

Audacious Philanthropy

Lessons from 15 World-Changing Initiatives. *by Susan Wolf Ditkoff and Abe Grindle*

PRIVATE PHILANTHROPISTS HAVE HELPED PROPEL some of the most important social-impact success stories of the past century: Virtually eradicating polio globally. Providing free and reduced-price lunches for all needy schoolchildren in the United States. Establishing a universal 911 service. Securing the right for same-sex couples to marry in the U.S. These efforts have transformed or saved hundreds of millions of lives. That we now take them for granted makes them no less astonishing: They were the inconceivable moon shots of their day before they were inevitable success stories in retrospect.

Many of today's emerging large-scale philanthropists aspire to similarly audacious successes. They don't want to fund homeless shelters and food pantries; they want to end homelessness and hunger. Steady, linear progress isn't enough; they demand disruptive, catalytic, systemic change—and in short order. Even as society grapples with important questions about today's concentrations of wealth, many of the largest philanthropists feel the weight of responsibility that comes with their privilege. And the scale of their ambition, along with the wealth they are willing to give back to society, is breathtaking.

But a growing number of these donors privately express great frustration. Despite having written big checks for years, they aren't seeing transformative successes for society: Think of philanthropic interventions to arrest climate change or improve U.S. public education, to cite just two examples. When faced with setbacks and public criticism, the best philanthropists reexamine their goals and approaches, including how they engage the communities they aspire to help in the decision-making process. But some retreat to seemingly safer donations to universities or art museums, while others withdraw from public giving altogether.

Audacious social change is incredibly challenging. Yet history shows that it can succeed. Unfortunately, success never results from a single grant or silver bullet; it takes collaboration, government engagement, and persistence over decades, among other things. To better understand why some efforts defy the odds and what lessons today's philanthropists can learn from successful efforts of the past, we dived deep into 15 breakthrough initiatives, ranging from broad access to end-of-life hospice care to fair wages for migrant farmworkers in the U.S. to a lifesaving rehydration solution in Bangladesh (see the sidebar "Audacious Social-Change Initiatives of the Past Century"). Our research revealed five elements that together constitute a framework for philanthropists pursuing large-scale, swing-for-the-fences change. Successful efforts:

- Build a shared understanding of the problem and its ecosystem

- Set "winnable milestones" and hone a compelling message

- Design approaches that will work at massive scale

- Drive (rather than assume) demand

- Embrace course corrections

The role of philanthropists in these historical success stories varied. By and large they underwrote the efforts of others. The hands-on work fell, as it does today, to NGO leaders, service providers, activists, and many others on the front lines of social change. The common thread in these success stories was that philanthropists

Idea in Brief

The Challenge

Many of today's philanthropists aspire to audacious results. But despite having written big checks for years, they aren't seeing large-scale results.

The Inspiration

Historical initiatives ranging from the virtual eradication of polio globally to the legalization of same-sex marriage in the United States demonstrate that ambitious social-change efforts can succeed.

The Lessons

A deep dive into 15 successful initiatives reveals five common elements. Those efforts built a shared understanding of the problem; set winnable milestones; designed approaches that work at massive scale; drove demand; and embraced course corrections.

understood the importance of the five elements and were willing to fund any or all of them as needed. They acted as sources of flexible capital, identifying gaps left by others and directing their resources accordingly. Sometimes only minor support focused on one of the five elements was enough to tip the scales.

This framework does not constitute a simple or linear recipe. Real change is highly complex and driven by many forces, luck and timing play important roles, and causality is impossible to prove. Still, we believe that if ambitious philanthropists apply the framework over the arc of a campaign, they may substantially increase the odds of achieving transformative change.

The Challenge

Before we look closely at our historical success stories, it's instructive to consider some high-level reasons why so many efforts wither on the vine. Most of the initiatives we studied shared four important patterns: Success took a long time—nearly 90% of the efforts spanned more than 20 years (with a median of about 45 years). It frequently entailed government cooperation—80% required changes to government funding, policies, or actions.

It often necessitated collaboration—nearly 75% involved active coordination among key actors across sectors. And at least 66% featured donors who made one or more philanthropic big bets—gifts of $10 million or more.

Unfortunately, these patterns go against the grain of much philanthropic practice today. Donors know conceptually that achieving widespread change can take a long time, even for the most important and straightforward ideas. (As the physician Atul Gawande points out, the basic lifesaving practice of hand washing and sterilizing surgical instruments and facilities took 30 years to gain acceptance even after a leading medical journal published ironclad evidence in support of it.) Yet philanthropists often fund grantees with the expectation that much more complex change can be achieved in just a handful of years. Wary of red tape and of being perceived as "too political," many donors have been unwilling to fund work that meaningfully engages with the U.S. government, despite the central role it plays and the trillions of dollars it spends addressing society's toughest problems. Furthermore, collaboration of any type can be difficult and costly, so few philanthropists meaningfully support or engage in it, even though most are frustrated with the inefficient proliferation of siloed change efforts. And finally, only a small fraction of donor gifts for social change are large enough to make a dent—although philanthropists routinely commit $20 million or more to infinitely simpler challenges, such as building a university library or a museum wing.

To be sure, in none of our success stories could a philanthropist declare total victory. Despite near-universal use of infant car seats, children still die in car accidents. Despite nationwide access to free and reduced-price lunch, schoolchildren still go hungry. Despite substantial increases, farmworkers still have not achieved truly livable wages. But by focusing on the elements in the framework above, the movements' donors and change leaders enabled huge strides.

Let's look at the five elements in detail and explore how a thorough understanding of each can help funders pave the way for meaningful change.

Build a Shared Understanding of the Problem and Its Ecosystem

Everyone knows that you can't solve a problem you don't understand. The leaders of the successful social movements we studied appreciated and carefully framed the issues they sought to address. They knew who was affected and what forces perpetuated the problems. They often studied deeply entrenched racial, cultural, and economic dynamics, enabling them to attack root causes; figured out who benefited from (and would fight to preserve) the status quo; and built evidence bases that propelled action. And they revisited these questions as the problems and surrounding ecosystems evolved or as the change effort moved into new population segments, geographies, or other frontiers.

Consider the movement to reduce tobacco use in the United States. Decades of research funding, including substantial investments from the American Cancer Society and the Robert Wood Johnson Foundation, among others, were needed to construct an airtight scientific case that tobacco was harmful to people's health. The consensus that was built among scientists, doctors, government leaders, and eventually smokers was crucial to overcoming vigorous resistance and obstruction funded by Big Tobacco.

Still, getting people to break a socially reinforced habit involving a cheap, widely available, and chemically addictive product was extremely difficult. Recognizing the limitations of early smoking-cessation efforts, advocates continued to invest in research and problem reframing. This led them to modify their definition of the problem and pivot from smoking cessation per se to the broader aim of tobacco control.

To make it easier for individuals to quit, the movement refined the scientific and behavioral understanding of smoking as an addiction, facilitating the creation of products such as nicotine gum and patches. At the same time, it began to invest in changing the "system" of incentives and cultural norms that helped perpetuate smoking, resulting in laws to restrict smoking and protect the health of nonsmokers; significantly higher cigarette taxes; heavy restrictions or bans on sales channels such as vending machines; the outlawing of smoking in public places, advertising aimed at children, and ultimately mass-market advertising; and a decline in Hollywood and TV portrayals of smoking. Cigarettes eventually became expensive, inconvenient, and socially stigmatized, and smoking rates among adults plummeted from 42% a half century ago to 15% in 2015.

The best philanthropists understand that agreeing on the problem to be addressed is a seemingly obvious but highly tricky step, and they commission actionable research and policy analysis that foster consensus around why a problem persists and how to attack it. They also understand that such investments must be ongoing, because the problem and its ecosystem shift over time. Had antitobacco advocates relied only on the research reports commissioned in the 1950s and 1960s, their efforts might have been scientifically correct but largely failed. And note that cutting the smoking rate to below 15% is likely to require further research and reframing of the problem, because the challenge is substantively different, in much the way solving the "last mile" challenge in business (how to reach customers in the most remote or challenging contexts) differs from growing a nascent customer base.

Set Winnable Milestones and Hone a Compelling Message

Making progress is hard when the goal is big and vague; behavioral science teaches us that it's human nature to get paralyzed. The leaders in our case studies often kept people motivated and engaged by identifying concrete, measurable goals—what we call "winnable milestones"—and pairing them with emotionally compelling messages or calls to action. Honing an emotionally resonant message requires a range of activities, such as polling, message testing, and conducting focus groups, that lie outside the traditional scope for donors and are typically considered unacceptable "overhead" when they appear in nonprofit budgets.

Tim Gill and other philanthropists who support LGBTQ rights demonstrated the importance of setting milestones. In the early 2000s, at the urging of movement leaders including attorney Evan Wolfson, they began devoting considerable resources to the very specific objective of legalizing same-sex marriage nationwide. For decades the movement had focused on the broad goal of "advancing LGBTQ rights," and although that work continued, leaders hoped that a significant push on a concrete winnable milestone would more powerfully advance the larger cause. They further concentrated efforts on a targeted set of states in order to build momentum and lay the public and legal foundations for a national victory.

Leaders of other successful movements have similarly focused on concrete goals, such as "eradicating polio" (as opposed to lowering childhood mortality rates) and increasing migrant farmworkers' wages by "one penny per pound." But even so, those movements made little progress until they landed on core messages with emotional resonance—ones that spoke to the heart as well as the head, such as searing images of crippled children and harrowing accounts of farm-worker abuse. Indeed, the marriage equality movement struggled to connect with the general public as recently as 2008, even losing a well-funded ballot initiative in left-leaning California. In the aftermath of that and other setbacks, supportive philanthropists financed polling and focus groups to help movement leaders understand how to reframe the core message. The research revealed that many voters perceived the movement as driven primarily by same-sex couples' desire for the government benefits and rights conferred by marriage—and they did not find that a gripping rationale. This insight was pivotal: The movement refocused its communications strategy on equality of love and commitment, arguing that "love is love"—a message that struck a chord. Victories piled up, culminating in the 2015 Supreme Court ruling that legalized same-sex marriage throughout the United States. And although limited in scope, the push for marriage equality advanced the broader LGBTQ rights agenda in ways that might not otherwise have been possible or that would have taken much longer.

Audacious Social-Change Initiatives of the Past Century

WE STUDIED 15 SOCIAL MOVEMENTS that defied the odds and achieved life-changing results to uncover lessons for today's ambitious donors. Although we now take their success for granted, most of these initiatives took many decades to achieve breakthroughs.

The Anti-Apartheid Movement	The institutionalized oppression of South Africa's nonwhites came to an end in the 1990s—more than four decades after apartheid first became law—thanks to a tireless campaign of social, political, and economic activism.
Aravind Eye Hospital	Using a highly efficient surgical model and variable pricing, this hospital chain has reduced cataract blindness in Tamil Nadu, India, by more than 50% and serves all patients regardless of ability to pay.
Car Seats	By 2006, some 98% of U.S. children traveling by car were restrained in safety seats, reducing their risk of death in an auto accident by 71%.
CPR Training	More than 18 million Americans a year learn this emergency procedure, administered to nearly half the people who experience cardiac arrest outside a hospital.
The Fair Food Program	Fast-food boycotts and other efforts led by migrant farmworkers significantly improved working conditions and increased wages for tomato pickers in Florida and other U.S. states.
Hospice Care	This system of specialized palliative care, started in the late 1940s, now supports 60% of dying patients in the U.S.
Marriage Equality	A focused initiative of the LGBTQ agenda, this social movement culminated in the legalization of same-sex marriage in the United States in 2015.

Motorcycle Helmets in Vietnam	Helmets specially designed for tropical climates, along with a national helmet law and advertising campaign, raised rates of use in Vietnam from 30% to 95%.
The National School Lunch Program	By 2012, some 31 million U.S. children—more than half of all public school students—received free or reduced-price meals.
911 Emergency Services	Nationwide access to a trauma response system and other emergency services via a three-digit phone number was made available in the U.S. in 1968.
Oral Rehydration Solution	Widespread adoption of a sugar/salt rehydration mixture by Bangladeshi households resulted in a 90% reduction in children's deaths from diarrheal diseases.
Polio Eradication	Following the development of a vaccine in 1955 and decades-long inoculation efforts, polio has been virtually eradicated globally.
Public Libraries	Early investment by Andrew Carnegie, coupled with long-running advocacy by interest groups, has provided 96% of Americans with easy access to free libraries.
Sesame Street	The first TV show to achieve early-childhood learning gains, launched in the U.S. in the late 1960s, is now viewed by more than 156 million children around the world.
Tobacco Control	The long-term antismoking effort, started in the 1950s, eventually reduced smoking rates by more than 60% among U.S. teens and adults.

Design Approaches That Will Work at Massive Scale

A solution that doesn't work at the scale of the problem isn't a real solution. Unfortunately, billions of philanthropic dollars are poured into perfecting social services and products that are truly viable only for small numbers of an affected group—5,000 people, five cities, even five states. Such efforts are often local, entrepreneurial, or academic responses to unmet needs or low-quality, underfunded government services (a different way to waste money). But the "innovations" themselves are often too expensive, too complex, or too dependent on specialized talent to be viable at the extent of the need. And even when small-scale solutions are tested with larger groups, the leap is usually from, say, 500 people to 1,000—which reveals almost nothing. The real question should be whether an innovation that can serve 500 people can effectively serve 50,000 or 500,000 people.

Of course, designing a solution or a change strategy that works at scale is enormously challenging. Like any innovation process, it may involve many false starts. The key test is to determine what it would take for the proposed approach to be implemented at full scale—and then critically evaluate whether that is realistic. Often, simple math demonstrates that it is not. For example, if 10 million impoverished American youths need help getting into and graduating from college, and a high-quality program costs $5,000 per person, we need to ask whether any funding model, even one led by the government, could feasibly cover the $50 billion a year needed to serve them all. Could any police force realistically control illegal logging in the dense and gigantic Amazon rainforest? Can we expect that 25 million nurses across India will learn and reliably implement a 20-step procedure for sterilizing medical equipment? Do we believe that billions of concerned coffee drinkers will do their own research to make sure that their particular blend is grown under fair conditions? Those tactics might work at limited scope, but they're all likely to break down at the full scale of the need.

Still, cracking this nut is possible. All 15 initiatives in our study achieved impact at scale, although no two followed the same path.

Some did it by investing deeply in R&D and developing an innovative form of an existing product, program, or process; some found a breakthrough business model; some took advantage of an existing distribution system instead of trying to build a new one; and some hit upon one or more novel leverage points to influence the relevant field or system. Often, philanthropy is needed to support this kind of innovation and experimentation, especially for solutions that truly work at scale.

Consider Aravind Eye Hospitals. The organization was founded in 1976 by Govindappa Venkataswamy (Dr. V), an Indian physician who set out to eliminate preventable cataract-caused blindness among the 48 million residents of the state of Tamil Nadu. Initially financed by the "philanthropy" of Dr. V and his family (he mortgaged his home for start-up funds), Aravind developed an ultra-efficient surgical process and paired it with a business model based on a variable fee structure. Together these allowed Aravind to treat hundreds of thousands of poor patients at little or no charge by attracting enough paying patients to cover the costs for the poor. Now serving some 250,000 people a year—with quality equal to or better than the British National Health System's, and at one one-thousandth of the cost—Aravind has propelled a dramatic drop in the rate of blindness throughout Tamil Nadu and has expanded to serve and share its model in other regions as well.

Consider also the lifesaving technique known as CPR, which achieved widespread adoption in the United States thanks to its "product" innovation. The leaders of the movement relied on significant simplification of the technique—work funded largely by research and local philanthropic grants—so that almost any layperson could remember and perform it. This enabled it to be picked up and broadly disseminated through massive existing distribution channels. Beginning in 1975, the American Red Cross incorporated CPR into its network of first aid, workplace safety, and lifeguarding courses; the American Heart Association soon followed. Today more than 18 million Americans, including many high school students taking health classes, are trained in CPR every year, and the procedure is administered to almost 50% of people who experience cardiac arrest outside a hospital, doubling or tripling their chances of survival when performed within the first few minutes.

Finally, in a David-versus-Goliath triumph, a group of migrant farmworkers in Florida—who pick almost all the winter tomatoes in the United States—hit upon a scalable model and leverage point to gain humane working conditions and a 70% increase in wages. This wasn't simple or quick; it required years of trial and error. For decades the workers had endured wage theft, verbal and physical abuse, racial discrimination, and sexual harassment in the course of punishing 70- to 80-hour workweeks—and for earnings amounting to just $10,000 or so a year. In 1996, when a worker was badly beaten by his crew leader for asking to take a water break, the community had had enough. A group called the Coalition of Immokalee Workers (CIW) responded for years with protests, hunger strikes, and a 234-mile march along a major highway to try to pressure farmers into improving conditions.

These actions had little effect. But CIW, aided by modest local philanthropy, a few faith-based funders, and the Public Welfare Foundation, continued to experiment until it found a strategy with the potential to affect the problem at scale: applying grassroots pressure to consumer-facing bulk purchasers of tomatoes, such as fast-food restaurants. These companies were much more vulnerable than growers to pressure tactics, because their clientele was the public. With the support of other grassroots networks, including the Student/Farmworker Alliance and Interfaith Action, CIW launched a series of fast-food boycotts, starting with Taco Bell.

From 2002 to 2005, CIW and allies at 22 universities and high schools nationwide ended sponsorships and removed or blocked the opening of Taco Bell restaurants on their campuses. They launched campaigns in dozens of other communities as well. The pressure tactics worked: Taco Bell's parent company, Yum! Brands, agreed to pay growers an additional penny per pound of tomatoes to go directly to workers' wages; it also agreed to require that its growers adhere to humane working standards and allow monitoring by an independent nonprofit entity. With increasing philanthropic support from national funders such as the Kresge, Kellogg, and Ford foundations, CIW extended the boycott to other companies, and over the next few years it won the support of McDonald's, Subway, Burger King, and Whole Foods, along with food service providers Bon Appétit, Compass, Aramark, and Sodexo. In 2010 the growers agreed to raise wages and improve working conditions. The reforms have since been adopted by growers as far away as New Jersey and agreed to by chains including Walmart, Stop & Shop, Giant, and Trader Joe's. The movement's success has been celebrated by the White House and the United Nations.

The best funders understand that effectiveness and scalability must be equals. Rather than incrementally growing a small-scale strategy or solution, a donor may get more bang for the buck by patiently supporting grantees in rigorous R&D and testing until they discover an approach that works at scale.

Drive (Rather than Assume) Demand

Even if you build it, they may not come. The philanthropists behind our successful case studies realized this. So they invested in solutions that users and partners actually wanted. They funded robust sales and marketing efforts to support their ambitious goals. They supported the creation of new government requirements or regulations. And they ensured strong distribution networks that helped drive uptake by providing easy access.

Consider the effort to reduce traffic fatalities in Vietnam by encouraging the use of motorcycle helmets—a campaign funded in large part by Chuck Feeney's Atlantic Philanthropies. One of Atlantic's first grants of the campaign went to the Asian Injury Prevention Foundation, in 2000. Although motorcycle helmets had been around for a long time, AIPF's founder, Greig Craft, believed that the inappropriate design of existing helmets for tropical climates contributed to the very low rates of use in Vietnam. Atlantic provided $1.5 million to help launch a factory to manufacture lightweight, well-ventilated helmets specifically for the tropics. With this new solution in hand and a shared understanding of the problem thanks to philanthropically funded research and cross-sector working groups, Vietnam's

National Assembly drafted a new law mandating helmet use. Before the law took effect, AIPF helped mobilize funders to back a huge advertising push that used TV, billboards, sides of buses, and other channels to help educate and change behavior among the public. The campaign, which was based on best practices from other parts of the world, achieved a breakthrough relatively quickly: According to the World Health Organization, rates of use jumped almost immediately after the helmet law took effect, in 2007, from less than 30% to roughly 95%, and have stayed relatively constant since.

Significant investments in demand generation also contributed to the scaling of a simple, affordable intervention that has saved millions of lives in Bangladesh. As recently as the 1980s, dehydration from diarrheal diseases caused 20% of the deaths of children under the age of five, killing hundreds of thousands of children each year. That was despite the availability of a cheap and highly effective oral-rehydration solution consisting of nothing more than a precise mixture of sugar, salt, and water, developed more than a decade earlier by researchers in Dhaka. The government had distributed packets of the solution to its clinics across the country, but most sat on the shelf, unused. The problem was twofold: The solution was not in keeping with long-held cultural beliefs about treatment, and government clinics were rarely used in rural areas—more than 80% of Bangladeshi mothers relied instead on traditional healers, village health volunteers, and other informal providers for their health needs.

Two major donor-funded efforts helped turn things around. Starting in 1980, several aid agencies and international NGOs invested more than $22 million (in 2016 dollars) in a 10-year education campaign run by the Bangladesh-based NGO BRAC. The campaign trained thousands of local women to mix the solution and sent them door-to-door to teach more than 12 million households about the lifesaving treatment. And in 1983, USAID began a multimillion-dollar funding of the Social Marketing Company, a local social enterprise incubated by Population Services International, to mass-produce, market, and sell the packets. To meet the distribution challenge and further drive demand, SMC built connections with the thousands of unlicensed health-care providers who served most Bangladeshi families. It also secured partnerships with private distributors, who by 2007 had brought the packets to 91% of the country's pharmacies and 32% of its grocery stores. Today the solution is used by 80% of Bangladeshi households, and children's deaths from diarrheal diseases have plummeted by 90%.

Finally, let's look at *Sesame Street*. In the late 1960s, the Carnegie Corporation's vice president, Lloyd Morrisett, commissioned television producer Joan Ganz Cooney to explore the then-revolutionary concept of early learning for children via television. The two collaborated on an ambitious budget for the initial season: roughly $55 million (in 2016 dollars). Cooney advocated investing in strong design, including hiring a leading children's entertainment producer—thus boosting the odds that the show would resonate with its target beneficiaries. She pushed for ongoing research to test how well the program captured children's attention and improved their learning. And a significant share of the budget—8%—was earmarked for publicity and outreach.

Morrisett secured a $7 million contribution from Carnegie and raised the rest from other philanthropies and the government. *Sesame Street* succeeded spectacularly. In its first week, more than 1.5 million children tuned in—twice the number of children attending preschool. Within a year the program was reaching 36% of all preschool-aged children; by 1993 the figure was 77%. Today *Sesame Street* is viewed by more than 156 million children around the world, and numerous studies have demonstrated that it significantly advances early learning, contributing to a rise in similar programming by other broadcasters.

Embrace Course Corrections

Every long-haul effort hits roadblocks. To achieve winnable milestones over decades, funders need to support their grantees' capacity to continuously improve. Experienced funders recognize that challenges may differ by context (urban versus rural versus last mile) and population segment (early adopters versus laggards) and that social-impact organizations need to experiment, measure, and adapt as those factors change. But only a handful of philanthropists today invest deeply in creating the space and infrastructure for grantees to learn, adjust, and at times fail. Patience is limited, and what little money is earmarked for measurement and evaluation too often prioritizes accountability and attribution of credit rather than learning for continuous improvement.

Course corrections were important in all the stories above. Recall the numerous setbacks suffered by the marriage equality movement; because donors were patient, it could learn from those setbacks and ultimately discover a winning strategy. Philanthropy played a smaller but still critical role in the course correction of another initiative: the National School Lunch Program. The concept of school lunches for poor children had been around since the early 1900s, and the federal government had subsidized them since the Depression. Many saw the effort as a great success. But the Field Foundation of New York continued to invest in research into the issue, and in 1968 two reports illuminated the depths of hunger that still existed and the terrible gaps in the program's coverage, galvanizing the public, Congress, and the president to renew their focus. Over the next two years the government amended the program. Among other things, it established federal guidelines for eligibility (rather than leaving that to local school districts), shifted the emphasis toward helping the needy rather than subsidizing lunch for all students, and increased funding. By 2012, some 31 million children a day—more than half of all public school students—were receiving free or reduced-price meals. Although issues of access have not been fully resolved— advocates are continuing to work on destigmatizing delivery and increasing adoption by children themselves—the improvements have been dramatic.

For the types of social challenges targeted by audacious philanthropists and other change makers, adaptation informed by robust measurement is key. To fuel progress, funders need to make sure that both their attitudes and their funding reflect that reality.

The Past as Prologue

What can today's most ambitious philanthropists learn from those who helped solve big, important problems in the past? At the highest level, the successful strategies we uncovered ran counter to prevailing funding practices. They included decades-long persistence, even when the pace of change felt slow; financial support for collaboration among key actors, even when it meant giving up some control; engagement with governments to influence funding and action, even in uncertain times; and big philanthropic bets that shifted power from the donor to the doers and beneficiaries.

The issues most deserving of investment today are different from those of past decades; what remains constant is the need for shared and dynamic problem definition, clear and winnable milestones, solutions built for scale, robust investments to drive and serve demand, and adaptive capacity among philanthropists and grantees alike. Understanding and acting on these elements can help funders achieve the audacious successes they seek.

Originally published in September—October 2017. Reprint R1705J

MICHELLE BACHELET was the first woman to be elected President of Chile and served two terms. She is now UN High Commissioner for Human Rights.

ALISON BEARD is a senior editor at *Harvard Business Review*.

KATHERINE BELL was editor of HBR.org.

ARTHUR C. BROOKS is the president of the American Enterprise Institute.

RICHARD P. CHAIT is a professor emeritus at Harvard University's Graduate School of Education.

FRÉDÉRIC DALSACE is an associate professor of marketing and holds the Social Business, Enterprise and Poverty chair at HEC Paris.

J. GREGORY DEES was a professor of management at Duke University's Fuqua School of Business. A pioneer in the field of social entrepreneurship, he helped launch Stanford's Center for Social Innovation and was the founding faculty director of Duke's Center for the Advancement of Social Entrepreneurship.

SUSAN WOLF DITKOFF is a partner at the Bridgespan Group and the cohead of its philanthropy practice.

PETER F. DRUCKER was a writer, consultant, and professor of social science and management at Claremont Graduate University in California. His thirty-nine books have been published in more than seventy languages. He founded the Peter F. Drucker Foundation for Nonprofit Management, and counseled thirteen governments, public services institutions, and major corporations.

BÉNÉDICTE FAIVRE-TAVIGNOT is an affiliate professor at HEC Paris and the academic director of its master's program in sustainable development.

ABE GRINDLE is a manager at the Bridgespan Group.

THOMAS P. HOLLAND is Professor Emeritus in the School of Social Work at the University of Georgia, where he helped found the UGA Institute for Nonprofit Management.

JOSEPH HOOLEY is the CEO of State Street.

BILL T. JONES is a choreographer and dancer. He is Artistic Director of New York Live Arts.

SOHEL KARIM is a cofounder and the managing director of Socient Associates, a social enterprise consulting firm.

SALMAN KHAN is the founder and Executive Director of Khan Academy.

DANA LISSY is Editorial Production Director at *Harvard Business Review*.

WYNTON MARSALIS is a prolific recording artist and composer. He founded Jazz at Lincoln Center in 1987.

DANIEL McGINN is a senior editor at *Harvard Business Review*.

DAVID MENASCÉ is the managing director of Azao, a consulting company specializing in social business, and an affiliate professor at HEC Paris.

GEORGE MITCHELL served three terms as a US Senator from Maine. He was Majority Leader of the Senate in his final term and later served as United States Special Envoy for Northern Ireland.

V. KASTURI RANGAN is the Malcolm P. McNair Professor of Marketing at Harvard Business School and a cofounder and cochair of the HBS Social Enterprise Initiative.

SHERYL K. SANDBERG is COO of Facebook and author of *Lean In: Women, Work, and the Will to Lead* and coauthor, with Adam Grant, of *Option B: Facing Adversity, Building Resilience, and Finding Joy.*

DWAYNE SPRADLIN is CEO of Buzz Points, Inc. Previously, he was the president and CEO of InnoCentive, an online marketplace that connects organizations with freelance problem solvers in a multitude of fields.

BARBARA E. TAYLOR was a senior associate at the Academic Search Consultation Service in Washington, D.C., and a trustee of Wittenberg University in Springfield, Ohio.

DESMOND TUTU is the former Archbishop of Cape Town and the winner of the 1984 Nobel Peace Prize.

MUHAMMAD YUNUS, the founder of Grameen Bank, a microfinance business that first operated in rural Bangladesh, won the 2006 Nobel Peace Prize.

Index